# Advance praise

Experienced investors tend to forget what it's like to begin a dividend investing portfolio. David Bressler is different. His book is a practical guide to buying your first shares and learning how to value the income you receive as a shareholder. He also shares how dramatic the results can be, even for people who have never invested before.

—BEN REYNOLDS, FOUNDER OF THE SURE DIVIDEND INVESTMENT NEWSLETTER

Almost half of all women consider themselves less knowledgeable than men when it comes to investing. It's a perception that can drastically limit their ability to build meaningful wealth. Author David Bressler addresses this lack of confidence head on. He breaks down the obstacles, real or perceived, that can get in the way of successful investing and instead offers a simple four-step strategy. The result is a highly readable guide to confidently building wealth.

—FAITH POPCORN, FOUNDER AND CEO, FAITH POPCORN'S BRAINRESERVE

If you're a first-time investor looking to set up a solid financial future, allow David Bressler to take you by the hand and lead you there. By masterfully weaving together anecdote and financial insight, Bressler makes his book your ticket to creating financial independence—even if your only plan at the moment is to survive from one paycheck to the next.

—NATHAN RICHARDSON, FORMER GM OF YAHOO! FINANCE AND CEO OF TRADEIT

David Bressler is what I think of as a socially driven financial coach. His book is as much a call to action for a more equal, socially just, and green world as it is an investment guide. He not only maps out how to plan for a solid financial future he talks how about to do it in a way that aligns with your desire to do good. Call it conscious investing. Go ahead and buy Bressler's book—I don't see how you can lose.

—HAMILTON SOUTHER, TRANSFORMATIONAL COACH AND FOUNDER OF THE WHITE MORPHO INSTITUTE

David Bressler has a problem with the way most of us learn about personal finance: We don't. He's tackled this failure by drawing on innovative approaches to making financial planning both easy to understand and doable. He urges us, for instance, to think of investing as akin to launching a start-up, which makes the whole process way more fun—in case the idea of building wealth isn't incentive enough!

—BRIAN ROEMMELE, CO-HOST OF *AROUND THE COIN* PODCAST AND PAYMENTS INDUSTRY VETERAN

If there's one book freelancers should read in the next month, it's *The Elephant in the Room Has a Paycheck*, by David Bressler. The storytelling in the book alone is worth it, but the financial education that they'll receive—using a novel paradigm—is what they'll treasure. Freelancers like the freedom that comes with their work, but they'll love the freedom that comes with this plan for building their personal wealth. I trust no one more than Bressler to tell this story.

—CHRIS LEMA, VP OF PRODUCTS AND INNOVATION, LIQUID WEB

People are often enthusiastic about money, less so about finances. It takes a special kind of creativity to make the details of finances enjoyable enough that people will want to stick to their plans and reach their goals. David has done just that by creating an investing blueprint that's approachable and fun without sacrificing results.

—ALGIRDAS UNGUVAITIS, CEO AT JUMSOFT (MAKER OF THE MONEY PERSONAL FINANCE APPLICATION)

# The Elephant in the Room
# Has a Paycheck

# The Elephant in the Room Has a Paycheck

A fun and socially conscious plan
to get you started investing

DAVID BRESSLER

Infinite Probabilities
New York, New York

Publisher's Cataloging-in-Publication

Bressler, David, 1967- author.
The elephant in the room has a paycheck: a fun and socially conscious plan to get you started investing / David Bressler.
pages cm

LCCN 2016918692
ISBN 978-0-9969075-3-8 (hardback)
ISBN 978-0-9969075-2-1 (paperback)
ISBN 978-0-9969075-0-7 (Kindle)
ISBN 978-0-9969075-1-4 (epub)

1. Investments--United States--Handbooks, manuals, etc.
2. Stocks--United States--Handbooks, manuals, etc.
3. Portfolio management--United States--Handbooks, manuals, etc.
4. Finance, Personal--United States--Handbooks, manuals, etc.
5. Handbooks and manuals.
I. Title.

HG4527.B66 2016
332.67'8
QBI16-900082

Edited by
Christine Moore, NY Book Editors

Cover Design by
Michelle Holford & Marschall Design, Stone Pier Productions

Interior Design by
Marschall Design, Stone Pier Productions

Infinite Probabilities books may be purchased for educational, business, or sales promotional use. Please contact the Special Markets Department at service@elephantspaycheck.com, 646-479-5443.

Infinite Probabilities
New York, NY

*For Vanessa, Reed, and Evie*

"To love a person is to learn
the song that is in their heart,
and to sing it to them when
they have forgotten."

—ARNE GARBORG, 1851-1924

# CONTENT

# CONTENT

# The Elephant in the Room Has a Paycheck

# Getting the most out of this book

Many of my stories and teaching strategies have been developed over time to help people on their journey towards wealthy living. Here are a few addition resources available to readers that will both insure you have the latest tools at your disposal and make reading *The Elephant in the Room Has a Paycheck* more rewarding:

**1. Stay connected.** Please sign up for our email newsletter at ElephantsPaycheck.com/subscribe to help further your practical investing education and for tips on how to stay motivated on your journey.

**2. Download a portfolio tracker spreadsheet.** You can download a template spreadsheet to help you track your own portfolio and view the sample portfolio that was created when I started writing this book at ElephantsPaycheck.com/sample-portfolio. You can also see all the posts written to help you make these tools your own.

**3. Check in for updates.** I'll continue adding updates, support materials, and other information that can enhance your reading experience at ElephantsPaycheck.com/book-notes, including digital copies of the worksheets mentioned in the book.

Please stay in touch and let me know how it's going, and if I can help. You can reach me anytime at **db@elephantspaycheck.com**. I'll do my best to get back to you personally and in a timely matter.

Considering that it's often easier to stick with a plan like the Elephant's Paycheck Blueprint as a team, I'd also love to come speak to your community. If after reading this book you find that you have enjoyed it and the way I tell a story, please consider inviting me to speak at your next group, business, or non-profit event.

# Preface

I knew that I had this book inside me. I just never knew what it was waiting for before coming out.

It turns out, it was waiting for my wife. She gave me the human perspective that makes this book compelling—that "people" element that keeps this book focused on what matters to the reader. With her in mind, I was able to create a story that's easy to read and educates—something that's both fun and prescriptive.

*Have you ever felt like you should be saving more for the future, but didn't know where to start?*

*Do you feel that the advice your brokerage firm is giving you doesn't quite resonate with your situation?*

*Have you ever felt overwhelmed by "getting started investing" tomes full of math that never once tell you anything practical? Books that give you choice after choice, without a word of advice on how to narrow your choices—or a simple "how to"?*

It's challenging for experts to relate to "regular people" who don't have the same experience or education as the expert. Frankly, I felt the same way about the situation in technology, where I started my career. The people that create your software can't quite understand why you don't know to use it like they do.

The news media doesn't help either since it seems like financial news sites are run by ESPN producers. Financial news has become loud, obnoxious, and fear-driven. Those reporting it make it seem as though every decision is a "game changing" one, and if you don't do something, anything, you're going to "lose the game."

It's simply not how investing as an individual investor works.

Making things simpler is where I excel. I begin by telling a story to help you internalize what you're learning so that it's meaningful to you. I help you find a perspective to redefine your investing experience and then show you how to start and how to stay on track.

Even if you've never invested before, you can start this book with as little as $250 and end owning part of a company. If your portfolio is larger—for example, you're rolling over a 401(k) into an IRA—you can follow this plan to understand just how well prepared for retirement you are.

A lot of what you'll read in this book will help you shift your perspective to change your investing experience. For example, if you're just getting started, it's as much about education as it is about saving. If you're investing $250, think of it as tuition for continuing education and just jump right in—dare I say, even have some fun.

I'll help eliminate the fear of starting down the road to investing in the stock market and will guide you in building a plan. I'll provide step-by-step detail on what you should do to get started. And I'll help you filter out the fear and anxiety driven sports-reporting-style financial news so that you can learn more about what matters to you for your investments.

Of course, it's not only about building wealth. The best plan won't work unless you stick to it. It's about the human behavior behind investing, why it's so hard to stick to a plan, and what we can do about it.

One way to see why people can't stick to their plans is to look at their habit in writing. Let's say you start a given month with $1,000 in your account. You save $200 during the month, but when you look at the end of the month you have $900 in your account. "Stick it out," everyone says. "It's good for you!" they shout.

But losing $100 isn't fun. And it's definitely not motivating.

*What if I could show you how to measure your success so that investing becomes fun?*

*What if I could keep you motivated enough to look for ways to save more—so that you'd even look forward to peeking at your monthly statement?*

That's why this book is different. I purposely focus on what matters—and *I make it clear why*. I use a metaphor to help you understand the Elephant's Paycheck Blueprint. You'll develop a satisfying mastery over your investing behavior and continue to learn more over time, without having to get an accounting degree or an MBA. You'll be able to create a plan that intuitively makes sense, aligns to your social values, and doesn't require you to become an investment manager on the side.

Throughout the book, I'll share the unique metrics I've designed to change your perspective. It's a change that will make investing fun, and will also make it easier for you to plan for your future. The investing techniques used in this book are as old as the market itself. The "innovation", if you will, comes through the story we tell and the measurements we'll use to reinforce the behavior we want to establish. Your money is yours; your fees are minimal, trending towards zero. That's part of the reason your broker won't tell you about this strategy—but I'll elaborate on that next in the introduction.

First, let's start where every story starts—at the beginning.

# Introduction

## MONEY MAKING MONEY

I'll never forget the feeling of meeting my first love. I don't even think I was ten years old at the time.

All I had to do was put money in a bank account, and every three months, the bank would give me more money.

I remember going to the bank for no reason other than having my passbook stamped with my new, *higher*, balance. (This was the 1970's, way before digital. You'd have something that looked like a passport, only the bank stamped it for every transaction.) I loved the idea of my money making money—of earning more without having to work more. (Though of course at the time, I was too young to work.)

## A GIFT WAS THE SPARK

I was thirteen when I received my first five shares of stock in a public utility. The utility paid a dividend, a quarterly distribution by the company to shareholders, and the account was set up to re-invest the dividends. That meant that instead of a check, I received more shares of the company each quarter.

As the number of shares I owned grew, so did the income they generated.

I was hooked.

The company's dividends earned me more than the interest on my bank account balance. Of course, that extra income brought with it extra risk. The share price could go up or down, where my bank account balance was always the same. As a utility, it was considered a lower risk than the broader stock market, which is why my parents' friends had selected it as a birthday present.

I would come to learn that with opportunity for reward comes additional risk. But risk isn't a black box. You can make decisions that in practice, if not in theory, lower your risk.

At that time, there was so much to learn. My thirteen-year-old mind had a lot of questions, for which I was finding very few answers:

*How should I invest so that I could earn more than I could just by working alone?*

*Could I invest in such a way that the income I earned from my investments covered my expenses without having to touch my principal? Could I do this for retirement, and retire early? Or for safety, should I find myself unemployed?*

As it turned out, the answers were—yes, I could. And, more importantly, *so can you.* I'm excited to share how with as many people as possible.

## MATURING FISCALLY

I've learned a lot since those first five shares—and the world has changed a great deal since that time. Savings interest rates are practically zero. Inflation is real, though official measurements show it to be much lower than you and I know it to be at the supermarket (or at the college bursar's office).

Wages, especially among the middle class, have remained stagnant from 1985 through 2015 (source: https://fred.stlouisfed.org/series/MEHOINUSA672N). In 1985, the median income was $48,761. If that income had kept pace with inflation, by 2015 (the latest year for which median income numbers are available) median income would be over $107,400 a year according to usinflationcalculator.com. Instead, the median income in January 2015 was $56,516.

Simply put, income is not keeping up with expenses or inflation—and that's something that should create a sense of urgency.

I invested using dividend reinvesting until the Internet bubble of the late 90's. People who worked in technology, like me, made a lot of money by 'taking companies public'. I earned a lot through two initial public offerings (IPOs; TIBCO Software and Aether Technologies) and by trading technology stocks and stock options. I thought that only beginners invest for dividends. I thought that I

> **When I focused on dividends, instead of anxiety about my trading, I found I looked forward to the reinvestments.**

knew something special about the technology market that would give me a leg up trading the market.

I was wrong.

The bubble popped, the stock market fell, and it turned out that my special knowledge wasn't really that special. It's easy to bet correctly when the markets are going up.

I also bought a home during that time. The mortgage broker who saw my monthly statements thought I had forgotten to give her all of them because the account balances were so dramatically different from one month to the next. I still have those statements as a reminder of my hubris. They also remind me to enjoy what I have, a lesson I learned a little too late but one that has served me very well as a dad in the time since. There are things more important than money, and its pursuit.

I had lost a lot of money by trading instead of investing. Even when I had successful trades, I had to pay over forty percent in taxes. The amount I spent in taxes reduced my overall returns, and made it difficult to find the next trade. Every time I sold a company, I'd be working with only sixty percent of what I had, trying to earn back the forty percent I paid in taxes just to break even. I was playing a professional game with amateur training.

I didn't like the anxiety this caused. Nor did I have the confidence that I was doing anything other than betting.

I spent about ten years shifting my perspective, getting over the opportunity I missed. I wanted to hold on because stock prices had to come back. But there's no "reverse law of gravity for stock prices." In other words, what goes down doesn't always come back up.

I put a lot of thought into how I was investing, and to what ends.

When I focused on dividends, instead of anxiety about my trading, I found I looked forward to the reinvestments. It reminded me of the ten-year-old me who used to go to the bank to have his passbook stamped with the pennies of interest earned.

It was very comforting.

The real eye opener came when I met my beautiful wife. Vanessa was (and still is) a typical investor—someone who contributed faithfully to her 401(k) but didn't like to look at the statements. Someone who knew she should be saving more, but didn't know where to start. She found it too tempting (and too disappointing) to just see her savings sitting there, not growing. However, she reasoned—how much did she really *need* anyways? It was easier to spend it than to think about the hard questions that come when planning for the future—questions she had no way of answering definitively, anyways.

I had to explain to her what I did, why, and why we should keep doing it. I wasn't a beginner with what would become this blueprint anymore. I was, however, *communicating* with a beginner. Anyone who's ever taught anything before knows that it's one thing to learn something—but a whole other thing to teach what you've learned.

My wife is incredibly smart, but she isn't drawn to numbers the way I am. In an attempt to have her embrace and understand the topic a bit more, I looked for a book that we could read and discuss. But every single one I found was dry and uninteresting. So I started to explain our results to her in a way she'd find engaging and motivating.

It eventually occurred to me that *I* should write the book I had hoped to buy for her—that is, a book for people who'd rather be thinking about other stuff even though they know this is important.

And that's what you're holding in your hands.

If you're an experienced dividend investor, you won't learn any new dividend techniques with the Elephant's Paycheck. What you will learn is a new *perspective*—one that is important, because it drives behavior and a sense of satisfaction as you progress.

By making dividend investing approachable for non-numbers-oriented thinkers, I hope to provide more people with access to its benefits.

## A METAPHOR TO FRAME THE BLUEPRINT

You will gain confidence and knowledge if you talk about your investing blueprint. Yet, in order to talk about the blueprint, you need to understand it well enough to explain (and defend) it clearly.

The more you talk about it, the more you'll learn. The more you are challenged, the more you'll make it your own.

The problem is that to many people, it's a dry, boring topic. Dry and boring doesn't help you relate to it. Go to the bookstore, and all you'll see are titles that talk about "dividend investing" or "income investing". Or worse, titles that mention DRIPs (industry jargon that stands for 'dividend reinvestment plans'—I'll explain more about these plans in part two). Believe me—if you go to a party and talk about investing the way those books do, you won't be invited back[1].

Where does all the boring talk leave us? Financial education isn't strong enough to give people the confidence to explore topics academically and apply them to their own situations. Combine that with the secrecy with which Americans treat money issues, and we're left with a bad situation. It's too easy to ignore the need to build wealth and too hard to break through from industry marketing into knowledge and action.

I've been investing the way that I do for over 35 years. Dividends along with the tactics of reinvesting, dollar cost averaging, and compounding have been around for a while. But because most people are bored to death by the details, those details present a barrier to entry. On top of that, the stock market works *against* building healthy investing habits by measuring the wrong stuff. The four unique metrics I present at the end of part three will help change your perspective and work to motivate healthy investing behavior.

---

[1] First-hand research results; you may have different friends than I do, though.

I want to tell a story that's meaningful to the readers. A story that makes sense out of the investing myths we all believe. I think of understanding personal finance as the elephant in the room. We all know it's a problem, but no one is acknowledging it.

*If we want to encourage people to understand the value of investing with a long-term perspective, why aren't there any metrics to measure success that incorporate time? How many people do you know worked hard their whole lives only to find they can't retire?*

I take that elephant and put him to work. My elephant brings home a paycheck—along with annual raises that you can count on. I hope you can relate to having a second (or third if you're in a two-income family) paycheck helping out.

## WHO IS THIS BOOK FOR?

This book is meant for anyone who knows they need to plan for their future, but doesn't know where to start.

**Recent college grad?** Here's a great way to get started simply, even if you don't have a lot of money to invest.

**High school or college student? Parents? Grandparents?** There's no better way to learn than to have a little skin in the game. Plus, having friends or family to discuss this blueprint with is a great way to validate it in your own mind and make it your own. Parents, this is a great way to teach your high-schoolers about saving and investing responsibly. For grandparents, stock market investing is a great way to bond with your grandchildren, especially over a long distance.

**Freelancer?** Lucky you. Freedom to work on what you will, on your own schedule, until the day you die. Of course, this means that your long-term savings are your responsibility alone, and you've got to consider what your needs will be 10, 30, even 50 years from now. Time is your biggest ally; don't squander it. Start small, be consistent, and you'll be amazed by what you can accomplish without a lot of effort.

**Job switcher with a 401(k)?** Perfect. You have a good amount of money that you can't touch anyway; why not create an elephant that will work towards your retirement?

You may not have a lot of money to invest. No worries. As I mentioned in the book's Preface, can start with as little as $250. If you're working, I'd also recommend carving out a small monthly or quarterly amount so that you can see your Elephant's Paycheck grow even faster. I'll provide a clear step-by-step getting started action plan in part four.

## WHAT YOU'LL LEARN

I'm going to explain a basic approach using large public companies who pay dividends (don't worry if you don't know what dividends are; I'll cover that too). You'll be investing in the stock market, but in a less risky way than you might have heard.

You won't have to worry about timing the market because you're going to play by different rules. You're going to care about the dividends and only focus on companies who increase their dividends regularly. This helps you beat inflation and ensure as best as possible that the income your investments earn beats inflation.

As I write that, I have to make sure you keep one thing in mind as you're reading. Sometimes I'll talk in absolutes—like I just did when I wrote "ensure as best as possible"—but you must remember that *nothing is absolute* when investing. There's risk. With risk comes reward. However, we try to minimize the risk and stick to a plan so that we know how to respond to changes in the market or to our own circumstances.

With regards to absolutes, I often choose to define something in simple or absolute terms for the sake of, well, simplicity. As an example, in a few pages I'll tell you that companies pay dividends every three months. In truth, some companies pay them once a year. Others pay every three months but sometimes vary the amounts, or even pay special dividends irregularly. However, none of these variations matter for our purposes. In fact, they only confuse the reader about the very simple point I'm making: which is that companies exist that pay you something on a regular quarterly basis. If I were to try to give you every possible complication to every basic concept, it would make the book difficult to read—and it would not add a lot of value.

Having a plan also allows you to filter out the noise—of which there is plenty when it comes to finance. The crazy news and the crazier (but well-meaning) friends or relatives who have better advice often sow fear. We don't like fear—so we conquer it with a deliberate plan, measurable objectives, and by ignoring the stuff that doesn't matter.

The book is divided into two halves.

The first half provides the background needed to understand the approach and investing tools we'll be using in the blueprint. It contains two parts:

**Part 1. Investing in the Stock Market.** This part presents the baseline of information necessary to understand the blueprint. It covers the basics of investing in stocks and answers some common questions related to the Elephant's Paycheck.

**Part 2. Reaping Dividends.** This part gives readers the knowledge they need to understand the value of the Elephant's Paycheck and explains why dividends are the fundamental tool the blueprint uses for investing. I've specifically chosen to present the information in an understandable way that prepares readers to take action with confidence in part four.

The second half presents the blueprint; both the metaphor and the step-by-step action plan. It also contains two parts:

**Part 3. The Elephant's Paycheck Blueprint.** This part discusses the metaphor and dives into the human connection. It explains all the non-financial aspects of the blueprint, like motivation and investing in alignment to your social values. It also covers the practical considerations like beating inflation, managing your portfolio over time, and not trying to compete with professional traders. Finally, it introduces the unique metrics created for the Elephant's Paycheck Blueprint.

**Part 4. Putting Your Plan Into Action.** This part presents the step-by-step action plan that readers can take along with reading the book to create their own Elephant's Paycheck portfolio.

## The companies and individuals who most people turn to for financial education aren't motivated to share this sort of plan.

A common objection and question I hear is, *"How come no one else knows this? There must be something wrong; otherwise, wouldn't everyone else be doing this to make more money?"*

In fact, many people *do* know about this. There are countless books on the theory and concepts. However, all of them present too high a barrier to entry for people without a background or confidence in financial concepts and terminology.

The challenge with investing using a strategy like the Elephant's Paycheck Blueprint becomes that the companies and individuals who most people turn to for financial education aren't motivated to *share* this sort of plan. It doesn't make the financial companies money since there's not a lot of trading and no investing in mutual funds or exchange-traded funds (ETFs).

Broadly speaking, these funds are packages of securities (stocks or bonds) managed as a single product meant to make it easier for investors to achieve their goals while minimizing risk. Some funds are actively managed, meaning there is a financial advisor with a strategy guiding the funds investing activity. Other funds, called index or passive funds, are funds that track a financial benchmark like the Dow Jones Industrial Average or the S&P 500.

Actively managed funds are more expensive, but all funds have management fees that come out of the investment itself—and therefore reduce returns—every year. By comparison, owning individual companies often—but not always—involves small commissions on the transaction—buying and selling—but no ongoing fees over the holding period. In addition to management fees, funds often generate sales commissions for financial advisors, commissions that are absent when you purchase individual stocks.

With the Elephant's Paycheck Blueprint, you don't need to invest a lot to get started. If you're not investing a lot or buying commissionable products, the people who are advising you can't spend the amount of time with you that you need.

You'll also notice minimum account balances for trading accounts are often between $5,000 and $10,000. The Elephant's Paycheck Blueprint allows you to get started with just $250.

*Who's motivated to tell you about a cheap way to invest?*

No one.

*How are the people ~~selling you product~~ advising you going to hit their sales quotas if you choose a cheap way to invest?*

Precisely. And that's why people don't know about this method of investing, a method that's existed for decades.

The Elephant's Paycheck Blueprint is not about teaching a new dividend insight or method to dividend investing experts. It's about sharing a methodology that has existed for decades in human terms so that it becomes more accessible.

As part of making dividend investing more accessible, I've created unique metrics for measuring your results that speak to the long term, non-trading investor. These metrics encourage successful long-term wealth building habits.

## WHAT YOU'LL GAIN

**Safety.** You're taking control. You'll feel good about doing something deliberately towards your future. You'll get one of the most valuable assets you have in your favor—time—working for you.

**Mastery.** You'll have a plan with an explanation that makes sense. You'll set goals and objectives, and use a framework to make decisions about buying/selling.

**Elimination of guilt.** You'll know that you're taking some positive steps and lose the guilt about ignoring your future.

**Family harmony.** Couples fight most about money. If you're on the same plan, it's easier to discuss rather than argue. If you're teaching your children the value of money, you can work together using the Elephant's Paycheck Blueprint's positive results rather than making the conversation about rules and restrictions. If you're a grandparent, you and your budding grandchild/business-investor can imagine all the fun you'll have watching your company grow.

**A wealthier future.** The plan works and you're going to see the results. Stick to it, and your Elephant will contribute another paycheck to your household.

## LET'S GET STARTED

I'm excited to share this Blueprint in a way that's approachable for regular people, and something that non-financial experts can put into action in a way that puts them at ease.

Most books on this topic are too boring, filled with jargon, and much too far from practical to compel the average person to confront their uncomfortable savings habits head on in order to build wealth for the future.

I'm writing the book I wish *I* could have read when I was first exploring my ideas for building wealth by investing in the stock market. So I hope you profit from it—and have some fun along the way.

PART

# Investing in the Stock Market

The Elephant's Paycheck Blueprint uses individual company stocks as its main investment vehicle. That means you're buying a piece of an individual public company on the public stock market.

We target a very specific type of company; that is, stable companies that have increased their dividends yearly for over 25 consecutive years. These companies, called Dividend Aristocrats, are conservative companies with disciplined management. In the part two, I'll explain dividends. Briefly, they're payments the company makes to its owners (you!) every three months.

We also take the perspective of investing for a long period of time. While it's hard to define exactly how "long" this period of time is, it's certainly longer than 5 years—possibly much longer. If you're in your 20's and thinking about retirement, you're in a position to think in terms of decades, a length of time similar to the 30 year home mortgage common in the US. This focus and perspective reduce but don't eliminate the risk of investing in individual stocks.

You would certainly not want to create a portfolio based on this book with the money you're saving for a down payment on a home that you hope to buy in the near future—within the next five years. That said, the future is hard to predict. It's easy for five years to become ten, then fifteen. You don't want to miss the opportunity that time presents. (We'll learn more about that in part three.)

Of course, you'll see results sooner than five years. In fact, you'll see results almost immediately—within three months or less when you get your first dividend payment.

Chances are that you've gotten a lot of advice from others about (among other things) "diversifying your portfolio" or sticking to mutual funds to minimize risk. Some of the advice is good. However, most of it is incomplete.

This is because very few people put critical thought into investing and just repeat what they hear from everyone else. This just adds another barrier and more confusion about the goal that people should set out to accomplish—to build wealth over the course of their lives.

Let's begin by thinking about diversification and mutual funds.

## PORTFOLIO DIVERSIFICATION

It is a great idea to diversify your portfolio, if that's the financial position you're in. But, if you have just a few thousand dollars (or less—as we know, you can start your Elephant's Paycheck Blueprint with 'just' $250) to invest, a traditional approach to diversification—one where you buy different types of investments—is simply not realistic. By taking this approach, you'll be spreading your portfolio too thin.

Though this book isn't specifically about broad investment planning, here's a way to look at diversification and getting started investing: if you're not investing today and want to start, don't worry about diversification just yet. *First just get started.*

If you are rolling over a 401(k) or have a larger amount to invest, even a couple of hundred thousand dollars, most advisors will recommend mutual funds to diversify into instruments other than stocks. You can use a portion of your rollover for your Elephant's Paycheck Blueprint, and a portion for mutual funds that help you diversify away from individual stocks.

An even better approach is to use your new employer's 401(k) to help you diversify. If you're employed at a company that offers a 401(k), take advantage of it—because every 401(k) uses mutual funds. In this way, you can let your 401(k) be part of your diversification strategy. If you put your rollover completely in individual stocks and create an Elephant's Paycheck portfolio, you still have your whole 401(k) in mutual funds as a balance.

You can probably pick fixed income funds (funds that invest in bonds) and global funds (funds that invest in companies outside of the US) in your 401(k) to diversify further. If you keep an emergency fund in cash (as you should), you've got some great diversity between your cash, 401(k), and Elephant's Paycheck rollover. You have even more diversification if you own a home, because that's your diversification into real estate.

## A SIDEBAR ON 401(K) PLANS

You should be taking advantage of your 401(k) before using the Elephant's Paycheck Blueprint. Specifically, if your company matches 401(k) contributions, you want to contribute at least enough to take maximum advantage of matching. If you don't, you're leaving free money on the table.

After matching, try to put the maximum into your 401(k) while still also saving for the future outside of your 401(k). When you put pre-tax money into your 401(k), the money you would have paid in taxes instead goes into your portfolio. The money that you have in your 401(k) instead of giving to the IRS compounds over time. It's like the IRS gives you an interest-free loan that you can use for investing until you withdraw the money from your 401(k) (or rollover IRA).

When you withdraw, you pay the taxes that you would have paid back when you earned it (at your current tax rate, not the rate when you earned it). You also pay taxes on the money the loan (the money that would have otherwise been paid out to taxes) earned you, but you get to keep the rest. It's a good deal.

If you end up switching jobs, then you can roll your 401(k) into an IRA and use that money to create an Elephant's Paycheck Blueprint portfolio. It's still tax deferred money, but an IRA gives you full control of how to invest it.

The penalties are high if you withdraw 401(k) money before retirement (with rare exceptions)—so be sure that you can keep that 401(k) money for retirement.

## GETTING AND STAYING MOTIVATED

*Do you avoid looking at your statement balances at the end of the month?*

If so, the plan outlined here can help you get and stay motivated. As most people know, part of being motivated is being rewarded for good behavior. If we go on a diet, and see results in the form of losing after exercising and eating healthy, we're motivated to continue with those behaviors. The challenge with most portfolios is that good behavior has no correlation to the portfolio results. You save money each month, but your portfolio value might increase or decrease at month's end. If you aren't getting some sort of reward for this good behavior, building wealth won't become a habit.

With the Elephant's Paycheck Blueprint, we'll measure the paycheck your portfolio generates and the raises it gets (unlike brokerage statements today which focus primarily on the value of the wealth you're accumulating). Each new investment (and as you'll learn, re-investment) increases your Elephant's Paycheck. If you were to chart the paycheck—the black line in the chart below from the Elephant's Paycheck sample portfolio—it would go up and to the right, which is exactly what you'd want in order to reinforce the habit of saving/investing. Notice how the light gray line representing the size of the elephant is much more variable. This is because stock prices fluctuate over time, even as they trend in the right direction.

**Which line makes you feel better, the up-and-down variability in the 'size of the Elephant' or the consistency of the 'Elephant's Paycheck'?**

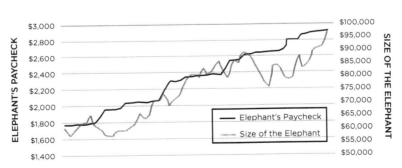

Figure 1: Chart of sample portfolio results highlighting the variability in the measurement of portfolio value versus the steadiness of measuring the Elephant's Paycheck.

Since most people track the overall portfolio value and not the monthly paycheck, the number they're watching is subject to the vagaries of day-to-day or month-to-month market movements. We don't get to reinforce the behavior we want to reinforce (consistent long term investing), since the up-and-down volatility leads to discomfort—which makes it difficult to stick to your objectives.

In fact, people tend to get frustrated and stop investing when the market isn't doing well, and get excited and invest more when it is. Look closely at this pattern and you'll realize that this amounts to buying high and selling low, exactly the opposite of what you'd want.

The Elephant's Paycheck Blueprint instead tracks the paycheck your elephant receives. The paycheck is structured in such a way that it gets raises and therefore goes in the correct direction—up and to the right as the black line in the chart above. The paycheck keeps increasing even in the presence of market volatility. Even if the stock market drops, you don't care.

Of course, certain things can work against us. Extreme events like 9/11 or the market meltdown in the late 2000's—even less extreme events like a warm winter or cool summer (for example)—will cause our energy and retail shopping behaviors to change in a way that affects company performance. That's where the risk comes in.

In general, it makes sense when you have good behavior rewarded and bad circumstances impact you negatively. What doesn't make sense is most people's monthly statements—where good behavior or bad circumstances seem to have no relationship to your portfolio's behavior.

When things make sense, we learn and adapt. When they don't make sense, we opt out—which is frequently what happens when people fail to see the money they've invested making them more money.

## MUTUAL FUNDS

Mutual funds play an important part in an overall investing strategy, a topic that is outside the scope of this book and not a part of the Elephant's Paycheck. Mutual funds give control over your investing strategy to the fund's manager (or fund strategy, if it's a passive fund). You don't get enough visibility into how the fund makes its decisions—or even the companies that the fund owns—in a way that would reinforce your motivations.

Without control, mutual funds operate on a "trust me" basis. You're essentially forced to trust the fund manager or strategy, and hope that it does the job well.

Trust and hope aren't great tenets of an investing strategy; at least, not if you want to depend on your investments to build wealth. If you're not motivated to participate, you won't be in a position to build wealth, regardless of what investments you have.

Motivation to participate is step number one, and most people overlook it. They force themselves to put money away (like in their 401(k)), watch it go up and down seemingly at random, and check out. They don't go the extra mile to save beyond that. We can see that in the way people cash out their 401(k)'s when switching jobs in spite of heavy penalties, rather than roll them over into an IRA. They've been so demotivated, they want to take their money and enjoy it while they have it.

Again, passive funds *do* play an important part of your overall strategy. But if you want to have fun investing (and you do, because anything fun you'll do more of) you need a better way. That's what the Elephant's Paycheck is.

When you do invest in mutual funds, pick low cost, index matching funds. The unfortunate challenge when getting mutual fund advice is that the people giving it are primarily concerned about themselves, not you. The individuals explaining the mutual fund to you are often getting paid a commission by the fund to sell it to you. At best, these ~~sales people~~ advisors are trying to maximize their commissions while finding you good investments. At worst, they're trying to maximize their commissions, period. I'm sure there's a gray area in between that represents reality—but *your* best interest is not their primary target. They're selling you something. It's good to keep that in mind.

How do you pick a good fund on your own? Warren Buffet—widely regarded as the most successful investor in the world—likes the Vanguard Funds. They're low cost and passive index tracking funds that are worth investigating.

## INVEST FOR A PAYCHECK—NOT FOR A PILE OF MONEY THAT HAS TO BE CONVERTED INTO A PAYCHECK

*What is your goal when you think about building wealth?*

A better quality of life is probably one of the key things. Security might be another; it's a big one for me. Retirement another.

In most cases, I imagine there's a lot of calculating what you'll need to spend if you retire, lose your job, or simply want to enjoy life more.

*If you invest traditionally, what gets measured?* **How much money you currently have.**

Using the amount of money you have as your starting point forces you to ~~calculate~~ guess how long that money will last and what you'll be able to spend in order to have a quality retirement. That ~~calculation~~ *guess* has to include inflation estimates and other guesses about how long you'll live and other stats about the future that impact converting a pile of money into a stream of income.

Sounds hard—not to mention inaccurate. Especially since attempting to predict the future is a loser's game.

The Elephant's Paycheck Blueprint allows you to actually measure and track the income your portfolio generates. There isn't any complicated guessing about what you can spend each year. Certainly, at some point you can spend some of the portfolio principle (the elephant). Since you're measuring the paycheck, you can plan to the income you'd like to have in retirement without any complicated guesses about inflation or how long you're going to live. And inflation isn't as big of an issue because your Elephant's Paycheck annual raises track to be larger than inflation.

There's a lot to unpack here—and you probably have some questions about things I've brought up in the last few paragraphs:

*Who pays the elephant his paycheck?*

*What are these raises?*

*How do we beat inflation?*

Part two will get started on answering these.

PART

2

# Reaping Dividends

Dividends are the basic tool used in the Elephant's Paycheck Blueprint. You will invest *only* in companies that pay and regularly increase their dividends by purchasing shares in those companies.

Dividends are what make up your Elephant's Paycheck. The companies that you invest in pay the elephant his paycheck through dividend payments. Selecting the "right" companies will allow you to build a paycheck that increases over time, because the companies will increase their dividends consistently and predictably over time.

Since you're trying to build long-term wealth and are investing in the distant future, you'll reinvest these increasing dividends in more shares to grow your paycheck even faster.

This paycheck is worth more than the one you earn at work, because dividends are currently taxed at a lower rate than regular income. The size of the advantage here depends upon your tax bracket, though—which is a discussion beyond the scope of this book—but here's a simple example: The current US federal dividend tax rate is 20%. For the sake of this example, let's assume that your US federal tax rate is 30%. Only considering this one tax for simplicity, $100 earned at your job is $70 in take-home pay ($100 less 30%). A similar $100 in dividend income, however, brings in $80 in take-home pay—because you only have to share 20% with the government.

Let's have a closer look to see what this all means.

## WHAT ARE DIVIDENDS?

When you purchase shares in a company, you become a partial owner of that company. When buying shares on a stock market through a brokerage, you're buying shares of a public company— a company that has offered shares to the public market as a way to raise money. You probably do business with lots of public companies like AT&T, Starbucks, and Ford.

Buying shares in a public company is just like investing in a local restaurant or buying shares in a startup—at least conceptually. You give the business money in exchange for a percentage of ownership.

Many public companies take all the profit and put it back into the business. Some return some of that profit to the owners (shareholders). Dividends are the return of that profit[2].

In the Elephant's Paycheck Blueprint, we narrow down our selection of dividend paying companies to a conservative group. We choose only conservative companies that pay regular and consistent dividends each quarter and have a history of increasing their dividends yearly. These companies are often referred to as Dividend Aristocrats, a term I'll explain more about later.

## BASIC DIVIDEND FUNDAMENTALS

I'm a big believer in understanding how things work. I think figuring out the "why" gives us confidence—along with the ability to keep that confidence when others challenge our point of view. In fact, many people I tell about the Elephant's Paycheck Blueprint respond with their own investment "strategies." Without a basic understanding of dividend fundamentals, I might lose confidence.

*When do companies pay their dividends?*

Companies that pay regular dividends usually pay them quarterly—that is, every three months. Some types of investments pay monthly dividends, and mutual funds often pay "distributions" two or three times a year on a well-defined but erratic schedule. For example, a mutual fund may consider distributions in January, October, and December, but only pay them under certain specific

---

[2] Writing about finance in a human voice can be frustrating at times—and this one of them. Many companies who pay dividends don't actually have profits, or pay out more than they have in profits. This is not always a problem, as profit accounting principles don't always reflect cash flow. For simplicity, I stated that dividends are a return of the profit—which you should understand is a simplified statement that is accurate enough for our purposes.

financial conditions (based on how the fund is performing). In this scenario, if the fund isn't performing according to these conditions, it may skip the October distribution. Dividend Aristocrats, on the other hand, pay dividends on a well-defined schedule—no matter the market conditions.

We prefer Dividend Aristocrats or similar because of their consistency. They give us the ability to plan ahead and stay calm about our investments. When what you expect to happen actually does happen, you gain confidence.

Companies that are similar to Dividend Aristocrats, but aren't, may be companies which have increased their dividends for many consecutive years, but not the 25 years required to qualify as an Aristocrat. Also, sometimes CEO's will publicly state that they intend to raise their dividends annually for the foreseeable future. While such a statement doesn't qualify them for Dividend Aristocrat status, it does make their companies interesting to us when creating an Elephant's Paycheck portfolio.

There are three regular quarterly schedules on which companies can pay dividends:

1. January, April, July, October

2. February, May, August, November

3. March, June, September, December

We'll get into specifics later, but imagine having companies in your portfolio on each of these schedules. Each and every month of the year, you'd be getting a raise by reinvesting the dividend.

## Ex-dividends

Ex-dividend refers to the timing of the dividend payment. The ex-dividend date is the first day after a dividend is paid. Investors who purchase shares on or after the ex-dividend date do not receive the dividend payment for this quarter. Investors use the ex-dividend date to know whether they get the dividend when they buy the shares close to the dividend payment date.

It's also an indicator of when the dividend is priced into the stock price. When the company pays the dividend, they're giving money back to shareholders, so the shares have less value (of the amount of the dividend).

Here's an example. Let's say a company announces that the next ex-dividend date is July 8th. The stock price is $50 at the end of trading on July 7th, and the quarterly dividend is ¢50. This is how it works:

- If you purchase the stock on (or before) July 7th, you are eligible to receive the dividend payment.

- If you purchase on July 8th (the ex-dividend date) or after, you will receive the next dividend payment (in October), but not *July's*.

- The stock price at market open on the 8th will be $49.50, because ¢50 has been given back to shareholders in the form of a dividend. In reality, the market is more dynamic than this, so the opening price might be different. Advanced traders might have their limit, stop, and stop limit orders adjusted (down by the amount of the dividend).

The ex-dividend date mostly doesn't matter for the Elephant's Paycheck Blueprint because we're not trading stocks; we're buying and *holding*. Any buying we do will likely be automatic and take place on a regular schedule. As such, our purchases wouldn't be affected by the ex-dividend date specifics because they won't likely happen around the dividend payment date.

### The payout ratio

The payout ratio refers to the percentage of net income paid to investors in the form of a dividend. A company that earns a dollar and pays a quarter dividend has a 25% payout ratio.

Sometimes payout ratios will be higher than 100%, which means that they will pay out more in dividends than they earn. This is not sustainable, but it's not automatically worrisome. You'd have to look at both numbers that make up the ratio and understand why they are what they are. Is the dividend too high or is net income too low? What if the company experienced a one-time "event" that negatively impacted net income? For instance—do you remember the Exxon Valdez disaster? The Exxon Valdez was an oil tanker that ran aground in Prince William Sound (Alaska), spilling hundreds of thousands of barrels of crude oil. It was the second largest oil spill in US history. It's a great example of a one-time event that affected Exxon's results. Once the effects of that event pass, the payout ratio should drop back to a more usual number. Companies like Dividend Aristocrats that value their dividend have contingency plans so that they can continue to pay their dividends and even increase them in the face of net income challenges.

As an aside, the Exxon Valdez spill occurred in 1989. The political climate has changed since then, and we can see the results of that change in the reaction to the Deepwater Horizon (British Petroleum) oil spill in the Gulf of Mexico in 2010. As a result of the Deepwater Horizon spill, BP was forced to discontinue paying its' dividend. It wasn't seen as "politically correct" to reward shareholders after such an ecological disaster. Were another Exxon Valdez-like spill to happen today, it's unlikely that the company's dividend would be unaffected even if the financials were otherwise healthy enough to continue dividend payments.

### The dividend yield

The dividend yield is the percentage return that the dividend yields. A 4% yield on a $100 investment is $4.

The dividend yield is an annual measurement. So in our example, our $100 investment would earn $4/year.

If you're calculating the yield, you have to make sure that you're using the annual dividend number. Some websites (like Google) list the quarterly dividend but not the annual dividend when they present stock information.

We calculate the yield by dividing the annual dividend by the stock price. Because the stock price changes each day—and each minute during the day—the dividend yield will also change.

In our example above, let's say we have a $50 share price and a ¢50 quarterly dividend. In this case, the dividend yield is 4% (¢50 * 4 = $2 annual dividend, and $2/$50 is 4% annual dividend yield). You can generally expect annual dividend yields of about 1% to 3% on Dividend Aristocrats.

## ELEPHANT'S PAYCHECK RAISES

The Elephant's Paycheck is a good perspective, but it's the raises that make it a great long-term investing practice.

Raises are fun, and they also importantly help keep your paycheck ahead of inflation. You know how it seems that things are always getting more expensive? How a movie ticket that used to cost, on average, $5.39 in 2000 cost $7.92 in 2013 (the latest year for which ticket prices are available as of the writing of this book). That's (mostly) inflation. If prices go up but your paycheck doesn't, you can't buy as much and your cost of living drops. When your raises outpace inflation, your cost of living improves.

The mechanics of dividend investing gives us three opportunities for capturing raises to our paycheck:

1. Reinvesting dividends; that is, taking your dividends in stock instead of cash

2. Optional cash purchases; buying more stock

3. Annual dividend increases; some companies have raised their dividends every year for decades, it's no accident

Let's look in more detail on how each of these works.

## REINVESTING DIVIDENDS

Your elephant has a very modest lifestyle. While you're in the process of building wealth, you don't need to use these dividends for anything but building wealth. So you reinvest them. Reinvesting dividends means taking the dividend payment in *additional shares* rather than cash. Doing so gets you a raise because the dividend payment following includes the new dividends generated by each reinvestment prior.

For example: you have $1,000 worth of a company. The annual dividend is 3% and so pays $30.00 in four quarterly payments of $7.50. Let's further assume, just for sake of illustration, that the stock price doesn't change. After the first reinvestment, you'll have $1,007.50 worth of that same company. At 3% (remember, the stock price is fixed to illustrate this point) you're now earning $30.23 per year (a raise of over .75%). Therefore, the second dividend payment is roughly[3] $7.56.

Let's follow this example through. After the second dividend payment—when half a year has gone by—you'll have $1,016.06 in company stock. The 3% dividend is now worth $30.48 a year, for a total mid-year raise of 1.6%. The third dividend payment will be $7.62, so your total after nine months would be $1,023.68. Your new annual dividend amount will be 3% of that new total, $30.71. The fourth quarter dividend payment will then be $7.68. Leaving you at the end of the fourth payment with a total investment of $1,031.36. Notice how you've received more than the $30 of dividends that we started out the year expecting.

After that fourth payment, your new dividend amount is 3% of $1,031.36: $30.94, which represents a 3.13% raise from the time of the initial investment. Remember, this is just one of three factors that impact your raise.

Later on, you're going to read about the annual dividend increase that you can expect. When you do your research, you'll see that a 5% dividend raise isn't unusual. Let's continue this example out of order, just because it's got an exciting result.

At the end of the year, you get a dividend increase of 5%. That means that the 3% dividend increases to 3.15% (3%*1.05). After

---

[3]Most dividend plans calculate to 4 or 6 decimal points; I'm rounding to two decimals here for readability.

THE ELEPHANT IN THE ROOM HAS A PAYCHECK

the first year in our example, your dividend payment will be 3.15% of $1,031.36: $32.49. That's a $2.49 increase from when you started. This might not sound like a lot—until you realize it represents an 8.3% raise. An 8.3% *raise* just for getting started. And remember that these raises continue year after year.

Consider this 8.3% raise in comparison to your regular salary. Have you gotten anywhere near an 8% raise at your job? Will you do so each year, year after year?

There is a small catch, however: if your Elephant's Paycheck Blueprint exists in a non-retirement account (in the US, that means if it's not an IRA), you're going to owe taxes on the dividends you receive—even if you receive them as shares. Under the covers, you're receiving a dividend payment and then buying shares. That dividend payment is taxable, and buying the shares sets your cost basis for the share purchase. The highest dividend tax rate (at the time of writing this book in 2016) is 20%.

In our example, with a $1,000 investment and a total of $31.36 in dividends for the year, that's a trivial tax debt of $6.27. If you're investing more, you may need to set aside money throughout the year and pay estimated quarterly taxes (at least in the US; other countries have their own rules). You'll want to consult a proper tax advisor on exactly how this works for your situation.

One of the things people don't like about investing this way is that you have to watch a lot of information—and keep track of each reinvestment like a new purchase. When you sell, you have to report each transaction, its cost, and sale price to the tax authority.

In truth, this was a lot harder before we had computers and before brokerages were required to track cost basis. Now, your brokerage should track this for you and report any tax considerations out for you.

This also speaks to another reason people don't consider this style of investing. The reporting done by brokerages is meant to help with corporate compliance and adherence to the tax rules. In other words—it's meant to help you pay taxes, not to stay motivated and build wealth.

*Why would you base your investment strategy on making it easier to pay taxes?*

We'll have a look at a few metrics that won't work for the IRS in part three—but will help you feel much better about the progress you make over time. These metrics are designed to keep you motivated to stick with your strategy, even through potentially unsettling market ups-and-downs.

## DIVIDEND REINVESTMENT PLANS

Companies will often allow you to purchase stock directly from them through programs called direct purchase plans or dividend reinvestment plans. These plans are designed for individual investors and are a throwback to a different era of stock investing.

In the early 1960's, when trade commissions were hundreds of dollars and investors had to buy "round lots" (trade in multiples of 100 shares—meaning the minimum purchase would be 100 shares), established public companies created dividend reinvestment plans as a way to offer the potential of stock ownership to individual investors. The 1990's brought the dawn of the internet, which enabled the opportunity for discount brokerages to offer self-service trading accounts and commissions under $20. Until that point, investing as an individual was expensive, almost prohibitively so.

Unlike traditional investing, dividend reinvestment plans were designed to enable investors to invest with dollar amounts. Investors could purchase as many whole and fractional shares as the amount invested entitled them to purchase.

These plans also had and continue to have low minimums, often between $250 and $500. You can setup recurring monthly optional cash purchases as low as $25-$50—all with no fee, or minimal fees. You don't need a brokerage account and you don't need to own shares already. They're a hidden gem for kids, students, and young professionals who want to start investing because they're so easy and so much fun.

They're designed for people to buy and hold company stock—so they have the balance of their fees on sale. The fee is still not high, but it's quite easy when you are ready to sell to transfer the shares into your brokerage account and trade on a discount commission.

Some people criticize these plans because you can't pick the time that you buy or sell as you would with a brokerage account; these accounts buy and sell on a fixed schedule. If you were trading stocks, this criticism would be valid. But since you're a long term investor who's trying to build wealth and maximize dividends, it's not a concern. When the time comes to sell, you can transfer your shares to your brokerage and pick the exact moment you wish to sell them if that's your thing.

Dividend reinvestment plans help small investors maximize the amount you can save over time by practically eliminating fees and commissions.

This might cause you to wonder—"So why doesn't anyone know about investing like this?"

*Why would a company tell you about investing this way if they won't make money from it?*

To find out if a company offers direct purchase plans just head to the investor section on their website. Poke around anything that looks like it's for "individual investors" or says "dividend". You can find some specific examples at http://ElephantsPaycheck.com/book-notes.

## OPTIONAL CASH PURCHASES

The second element of the raises you'll get comes from *optional cash purchases*, which are additional investments made over the course of the year. The phrase 'optional cash purchase' comes from dividend reinvestment plans, because often you can setup an automatic recurring optional cash purchase as part of the plan.

Outside of formal reinvestment plans, you can purchase additional shares any time you like. However, you'll pay a commission for the privilege. If you're going to add money to your Elephant's Paycheck Blueprint on a regular basis, you probably want to do it through a dividend reinvestment plan directly with the company you're buying to minimize commissions.

Either way, you'll get a raise with each purchase. While each raise might not be very much, it most certainly adds up over time. Remember our reinvestment example earlier? Starting with $1,000 earning a 3% dividend and reinvesting dividends quarterly we achieved a 3.13% raise after a year. Each investment *compounds*. That means that the dividends start to earn dividends, which then start to earn dividends—and so on.

In the part three, we'll see the "actual return" metric to give you a sense of how well this process of compounding is improving your Elephant's Paycheck.

## INCREASING DIVIDENDS

One part of your raises comes from reinvesting dividends. You get four of those a year, one with each dividend payment. A second part comes from optional cash purchases. You get a raise with each purchase.

The third and final part of the Elephant's Paycheck raises comes from annual dividend increases.

It's not enough for companies to pay dividends consistently. If they don't increase them consistently, you will lose out to inflation.

Not every company increases their dividends annually, but there are enough—there are about 50 Dividend Aristocrats—to form the basis for your portfolio. And they're easy to find.

Standard & Poors (known as S&P, a financial research company behind the popular S&P 500 index that is one of the top indices for tracking US markets) tracks an index of companies called the "Dividend Aristocrats®".

> *S&P 500® Dividend Aristocrats measure the performance S&P 500 companies that have increased dividends every year for the last 25 consecutive years and meet a minimum market capitalization and liquidity baseline.*

S&P tracks similar indices in Canada, the United Kingdom, Europe, and Japan if you're interested in investing in non-US companies.

The full list of Dividend Aristocrats changes infrequently. Their reliability over a long period of time is what makes them so attractive to Elephant's Paycheck investors. And while there's no guarantee to how much Dividend Aristocrats will increase their dividends, the increases seem to beat inflation over time.

Raises from dividend increases compare favorably to inflation, and they're just one element of three when it comes to the components that make up your elephant's raises.

## DIVIDEND ARISTOCRATS

It's cool to think about some of the Dividend Aristocrat statistics. For example, P&G has paid a dividend every year since 1890 (over 125 years), and has been increasing it yearly since 1956! *Can you imagine the world of 1890 into which P&G started rewarding investors with a dividend?*

The Dividend Aristocrats dividend increases contribute a large portion of our annual raises, and work to help us beat inflation. But they do even more—perhaps most valuable for our purposes here, they help to narrow down our choices of *where to invest*. Part of what makes investing is so hard is that there is a huge complexity to the amount of choice we have. Reducing complexity is a critical part of getting started and keeping focus on your plan.

I believe that Dividend Aristocrats informally reduce risk. This is a pretty controversial thought. There is a truism in investing and portfolio theory that there's no reward without risk. Mathematically, however, there's no way to account for ego (as an example). If you're the CEO of P&G, a company that has increased their dividend every single year since 1957, do you want to be the person that breaks that streak? Chances are, you'll work pretty hard to protect your reputation. And of course, the organization would support you because it's got the processes built into management behavior to plan for dividend increases.

A company doesn't do something for this many years without purpose, or raise their dividend for more than 25 years straight by accident. There's purpose and intent, and that serves us *and* our elephants.

From a theoretical perspective, these things might not imply less risk; but from a social engineering perspective, they do. The regular dividend raises combined with the company's dividend mindset allows us to practically reduce our investing risk over the long arc of time.

That said, companies hit rough patches. GE was a Dividend Aristocrat until the financial turmoil of the late 2000's. There will still be some risk. But, it's much more closely aligned to "what makes sense" than the apparent randomness of stock prices. When we feel that what we are doing "makes sense", it's easier to stick with the Blueprint and keep confidence in our strategy.

A final advantage to focusing on Dividend Aristocrats is that when a company fails to increase their dividend as expected, it is a good indicator of when to sell. Generally speaking, knowing when to sell is often trickier than knowing when to buy. Since we use dividend raises as a key determinant in filtering potential investments, the company is no longer an appropriate investment for our goals when it fails to increase the dividend.

## DIVIDEND KEY POINTS SUMMARY

Your Elephant's Paycheck is made up of dividends, payments made by the companies you own on a regular quarterly schedule. However, instead of spending the dividends, we reinvest them to increase the paycheck.

Speaking of raises, the companies that comprise your Elephant's Paycheck Blueprint portfolio are conservative dividend increasers. They're known as Dividend Aristocrats, companies that have raised their dividends each year for at least the past 25 consecutive years.

A third and final element of the Elephant's Paycheck raises comes from optional cash purchases, additional investments you can choose to make in your companies.

These raises mean that your paycheck goes up even as market volatility causes the size of your elephant to vary over time. Each company in the portfolio responsible for five raises a year to your Elephant's Paycheck (four for dividend reinvestments and one for the annual increase). Even when the market is volatile, you can look at your portfolio and see an ever-increasing benchmark—your Elephant's Paycheck—to stay positive and on track.

Importantly, these raises also help you beat inflation. Without beating inflation, you'd be fighting a losing game with decreasing purchasing power to your dividends over time.

It's possible that Dividend Aristocrats stop increasing their dividends, since there's risk to investing. It's important to remember that if a company makes bad decisions, and suffers as a result, and we lose money—while unfortunate, our brains understand it. While not a great thing to happen, it shouldn't impact our motivation to sticking with our investing plan the way normal volatility does.

A big challenge with investing for the long term—and sticking to it—is the seeming randomness to the stock market. When stock prices rise and fall for no apparent reason, our brains turn to fear and frustration. We stop looking at statements and account balances, or worse—we just decide to spend the money while we have it. But when you see the cause and effect, and a dividend is cut, we're less likely to throw out the whole strategy with that one company. You know when to sell and how to recover. Of course, we hope our whole portfolio is filled with companies like P&G that have increased their dividends for the past 59 years[4] and counting.

Finally, like a secret that brokerages don't want you to know, individual investors can buy stock directly from most if not all of the Dividend Aristocrats. Buying stock directly from companies minimizes costs and maximizes returns. As a result of the absence-of or minimal costs, it's also easy to set aside small monthly purchases. These optional cash purchases are a fun way to increase your paycheck over time (and get an additional 12 raises a year) and create a wealth-building discipline.

Dividend reinvestment plans usually have very small minimal account balances, between $250 and $500—which makes it easy to get started as a student or recent college graduate.

---

[4] As of 2015

## INFORMATION THAT CHANGES OUR PERSPECTIVE AND CREATES A NEW INVESTING EXPERIENCE

What do we do with all this information about dividends and aristocrats?

We create a blueprint. A blueprint is not quite tactical, but sets the framework within which we operate.

Our Elephant's Paycheck Blueprint will help you tell a new story about investing. This story is important, because it defines the boundaries within which we'll succeed, and helps to outline the behavior that will make us successful.

My investing story—this story—is personal. I share it, and I hope you can make it personal too. It started with a gift of five shares of stock and a personal wish for a book that could help me understand what I had. A book that communicated a human story, not a functional one. I held onto that wish for over 30 years—and when I got married, it clicked.

That "click" happened when I started explaining what would become the Elephant's Paycheck Blueprint to my new wife. My wife didn't know much (anything?) about investing. If I wanted her on board, and I did, I had to communicate in a new language. I had to tell a new story—one that would mean something to her.

It was through the experience of communicating to her that the Blueprint emerged. I'm sure you have questions similar to the ones she asked me at the time.

As I was writing and reflecting on my experience with my wife, I wondered broadly:

*Can we change our perspective about investing to help motivate us to stick with healthy investing habits?*

*How do we use these features of the market described in part two to create a plan that is easily understood and explained to others (so that we develop confidence and mastery)?*

*How do we track our progress and measure success?*

Part three will wrap the technical features we just learned into a human story to change your perspective. This new lens will completely change your investing experience—I promise.

# 3

# The Elephant's Paycheck Blueprint

It's no secret that most people consider investing to be a dry topic that requires math. This can be insurmountable double-whammy—even considering the importance of learning to build wealth. After all, we all know it's good for us—*so why can't we just do it?*

One reason is that there are a lot of barriers. So I use a metaphor with the Elephant's Paycheck Blueprint to break through the barriers.

This metaphor lets people internalize the behaviors we're trying to build, which makes the perspective that we need to develop feel intuitive (in spite of all the noise we see and read in the financial news world).

As kids, we learned through stories. I'm watching the movie Cars with my son these days, which teaches kids the importance of working as a team and considering others' feelings. There's more, and I'm sure you can think of stories you heard as a child that were meant as more than just stories.

As we got older and smarter, we switched to learning through facts and science. However, in this case, "growth" doesn't always serve us.

How many people read the facts on smoking or exercise from the comfort of their own couch while watching TV and eating ice cream? Don't they know it's bad for them?

Sure—but it *feels* good.

The thing subject matter experts often forget is that we remain human. Because of that, I knew that I needed to get in touch with the human side of our investing experience for this message to be different from the countless others you've heard.

Academics get us only so far as we try to build healthier behaviors. Facts and statistics don't tap into the human experience.

I thought I'd tell a better story using a metaphor. Not one with more facts and figures, though we have enough of those to support the story—but rather a story full of life—one with a little humor, a little perspective, and a touch of personal values.

## MY STORY

You've already read about how my wife and my own experience investing inspired this book. I'm an avid reader, and always hoped for a better book on the topic. I wasn't sure what "better" meant; but knew that if it had "dividend investing" in the title it wasn't going to have the right vibe, even if it was brilliantly accurate. I'd read enough of those to know that my wife—and most other people—wouldn't be interested.

In spite of that, I was in the bookstore with my wife in the summer of 2012, looking once again for a book that would help. I wanted one that explained how I set up her 401(k)/IRA rollover account just after she switched jobs, why I did it, and what it meant to her.

When I started investing with dividends (in 1980!) there was one good book on the subject, but it was boring. I wanted something better. In 30 years since I hadn't found that better book.

I was thinking out loud about how personal finance—in particular, saving money and building wealth—was so often the elephant in the room, the topic no one wanted to address but was there in front of all of us. I explained to her that I'd put that elephant to work. Now my wife's elephant was bringing home a paycheck.

And so the metaphor was born.

## A SIMPLE DEFINITION

The Elephant's Paycheck Blueprint is an investing plan designed to build wealth and meaningfully impact your life. It's quite a simple idea. Investing in Dividend Aristocrats to generate a "paycheck" is like having another income in the family.

As we know, the Dividend Aristocrats mitigate risk, provide inflation beating raises, and help us focus on something other than

## If you think "just don't look" is good financial advice, why not try to find something else to measure that keeps you engaged?

market volatility as a way to track our progress.

We then use two techniques—reinvesting dividends and optional cash investments—to maximize the Elephant's Paycheck raise. These regularly occurring positive and fun events serve to reinforce the wealth building habits we're trying to develop. After all, who doesn't like a raise?!

Along with these techniques, the blueprint contains some unique metrics to track progress. Designed to keep investors motivated, these metrics help participants take a different perspective than the traditional one, which focuses on portfolio size. They keep investors insulated from the *perfectly normal* market volatility and *insane* flow of fear-based news that's mostly meaningless to long-term individual investors.

### BACK TO ME AND MY WIFE

Neither my wife nor I wanted her to abdicate responsibility to me for her rollover. I believe very deeply that, like it or not, money is how we survive in the world and it's important for everyone to understand the basics—especially around family finances. It can't be just one spouse who is paying attention; both must be involved.

I'll never forget the time I was having a conversation about "the market" with my grandfather, and my grandmother chimed in. Imagine my surprise. I had no idea she knew what was going on; after all, it was my Grandfather who "managed their money."

I always had that example in mind. So once we got my wife's rollover in place, I'd keep track—but she would be involved, too. I created a shared spreadsheet so that she could look at any time. I even added a link to the spreadsheet her iPhone home screen and called it 'My Elephant'. And, I'd text her with things to keep her focused on the positive even when "the market" had a bad stretch. I'd remind her that her Elephant's Paycheck hadn't changed in spite of a market drop, or that the raise she'd gotten as a result of the market drop was larger than it might have been otherwise.

This helped me develop a perspective on the raise and the paycheck. Even when the portfolio went down, her paycheck went up. Remember the following image from the section in part one on getting and staying motivated? This image expresses what I learned from my wife. The motivation to invest is not going to come internally for many people. It's got to come from external rewards; rewards that have to overcome the negative reinforcement from volatility.

**Which line makes you feel better, the up-and-down variability in the 'size of the Elephant' or the consistency of the 'Elephant's Paycheck'?**

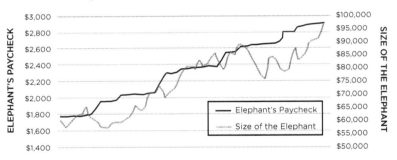

Figure 2: Chart of sample portfolio results highlighting the variability in the measurement of portfolio value ('size of the elephant') versus the steadiness of measuring the Elephant's Paycheck.

Volatility, shown as a light gray line, is normal and to be expected. The problem with volatility is that it often causes behavior that doesn't benefit us—that is, emotion-based trading that doesn't serve our long-term investing goals.

If my wife heard about the latest crisis on the financial news, I could point to a conservatively projected raise over 10%. She wasn't then, and isn't now, getting a 10% raise at work. Yet her elephant was and is, and has every year since we started. And, I made sure to update the spreadsheet with each reinvestment and dividend increase, and text her about it to celebrate. She could easily look at the black line, her Elephant's Paycheck, and focus on the fact that it's going up each month.

Over time, she came to internalize that she was making consistent progress toward her goal of having security in retirement. (Keep in mind that this is her rollover, so her goals with the account are narrowly focused on retirement because of tax rules. That may not be the case with non-retirement Elephant's Paycheck Blueprints.)

The contrast between market volatility and its impact on her portfolio size and the steady up-and-to-the-right progression of her Elephant's Paycheck is striking. It's a great example of the human element that most investing guides are missing.

Most people seem to assume that they way to deal with the ups-and-downs in their portfolio is to stop looking. But I prefer a positive instruction to a negative one. If you think "just don't look" is good financial advice, why not try to find something else to measure that keeps you engaged?

That's what the Elephant's Paycheck delivers: a set of metrics that you *should* pay attention to, in order to feel good about your blueprint and the progress that you're making. These metrics empower you, and you'll also use them as a way to learn what news to pay attention to and what ~~noise~~ news to avoid.

## YOU'RE STARTING A BUSINESS—NOT A PORTFOLIO

*It seems obvious in retrospect; so why does it work the way it does?*

This is a great question, and a topic outside the scope of this book. The short answer is that different stakeholders in "personal investing" have different objectives. The IRS wants taxes paid properly. So, they ask the banks to report on gains and cost basis. The banks use their statements to inform both the IRS and their customers, which in turn prompts people to understand their investing success through the information on their statements.

The thing is, the metrics you'd use for paying taxes are not the only one's investors can use. They certainly aren't metrics that help keep you motivated to invest.

You can help yourself by thinking differently about what it means to invest. Instead of thinking about buying and selling stocks, think about starting a side business—with, for example, $1,000 (the amount doesn't matter). With hard work, reinvesting profits, and eating nothing but ramen noodles for a few years, you grow that business into a company worth $100,000.

No one will ask: "What was your cost basis?" The story is that you started the business with $1,000 and now have a bigger business. It's an inspiring tale of hard work, sacrifice, and perseverance.

But, if you take that same $1,000 and invest it in the stock market while reinvesting the profits, no one looks at the "business you've built" in aggregate; they want to know your success at a transaction level of detail.

Why? In part because of taxes. Thinking about taxes has permeated the way we consider investments to such a deep level that we've stopped questioning *any other way* of measuring success— even when investors stand next to small business owners that are measured in a different, more rational way.

Up to this point in time, brokerages simply haven't thought about changing their perspective on reporting. In the next section, you'll read about user experience and investing. The tax-informed metrics brokerages provide simply don't account for a newer way of viewing their business' relationship with their customers—that of user experience. The right user experience can be used constructively to help investors develop healthy investing behavior.

## THE 10 HABITS OF A SUCCESSFUL INVESTOR

It's become quite topical to speak about "user experience"—that is, making a product more approachable. User experience accounts for both a product's functionality and the experience the consumer has while using it. Considering the experience combined with the function implies that function itself is not enough.

One place with examples where user experience helps to differentiate offerings is technology. Often, the focus with technology products is on technical specifications rather than user experience. For example, let's have a look at a product with arguably weaker technical specifications than its competition that captured over 80% market share from competitive products that beat it to market.

Consider the iPod. If we're just considering technical specifications, it was easy to find music players other than the iPod that would store more music (had greater storage), were cheaper, and that supported many different music formats. Yet the iPod became the market share leader because Apple considered the whole experience—what it took to get music onto the computer, easily sync it to the music player, and manage the music over time. These elements that Apple deemed most important really had nothing to do with the music player product itself—but rather how it impacted the *way people experienced* digital music.

Technical people for whom digital music technology didn't present a barrier to this day remain bewildered by the iPod's success. A music player is a music player; it should be judged based on the cost per storage size. Yet the iPod's success speaks to something else; namely, that people value the overall experience of the entire process, especially when the process entails specialized knowledge—technology in the case of digital music players, investing in the case of building wealth.

User experience is a dilemma new investors face when starting to build wealth.

Like digital music players, there are technical details—that of investing, the theories of diversification, of market dynamics, of risk. There's also the human side of things.

We're all smart enough to understand the functional details of investing. Unfortunately, we're often not *motivated* enough to build wealth even when we know how important it is to do so. The experience of getting started investing has barriers to the development of healthy wealth building habits. They're experiential barriers having nothing much to do with the investing product itself. Getting started investing can be intimidating, is often illogical, and it's hard to know where to get good advice when the people managing your money are living off the commissions of the products they recommend.

The Elephant's Paycheck Blueprint blends functional details with the human experience. Doing so creates a plan that people can internalize in order to break down these barriers to starting and sticking with a wealth-building program.

There are ten key characteristics that come together with the function of dividend reinvesting that make this plan fun, human—and hopefully something people feel empowered to explore. The next section will look at each of these in detail.

### 1. Developing good habits

Habit formation theory describes three elements that required to building a habit: the cue, the habit, and the reward. When the habit is positively rewarded, we develop a positive association between habit and the cue. When the reward is inconsistent, it becomes difficult to create a new habit.

For example, every month you have money deducted from your salary for your company's 401(k). Yet your balance is lower than when you started at the end of some months, even though you added money that month. *How rewarding does that feel?*

Let's take a closer look at this example to understand how the Elephant's Paycheck Blueprint takes a unique approach to solving this critical behavioral challenge.

The trouble with traditional investing metrics is that they don't reward the habit of saving money with consistency.

The habit we are trying to create is to save money monthly. Let's say that the cue is "you get paid", and the behavior is "put a little money away towards empire building." But if your balance is lower at the end of the month—even though you've added to the empire—you're not reinforcing your habit successfully.

It's not rewarding to have less at the end of the month when you have saved money that month (the habit). And this lack of reward weakens our commitment to the habit.

Many people who save successfully do so because they "know

they should" (an intellectual exercise) even when they don't enjoy the results (an emotional response). Anyone who's ever tried to lose weight or work out more can attest to how hard it is to think long term only on the basis of "it's good for me."

People need extra help to develop healthy habits. They need an emotional connection to the goal, not just an intellectual one. The Elephant's Paycheck Blueprint aligns the emotional response with the behavior we're trying to modify by changing the reward.

It's the nature of the stock market to express volatility, which makes it hard to stick to a plan because there's nothing on which to anchor your emotions.

Rather than looking at the size of your elephant (portfolio), the Elephant's Paycheck Blueprint uses the Elephant's Paycheck and her raise (past and future-expected) as the measure of reward.

When you save, you get a raise. Even just keeping the plan in place without additional savings added, you get a raise (in fact, you get five per year per company you own). You receive a reward for the behavior we want to encourage—thereby reinforcing your habit.

### 2. Have fun

Speaking of raises...isn't getting a raise fun?

*If you're given the choice of doing two chores—one fun, one not—which would you choose?*

Exactly! The fun one.

So just how many raises can your elephant expect a year?

At least five. Each time you save more, you get a raise—whether it's a dividend reinvestment (quarterly) or an optional cash purchase (monthly). On top of that, you get a dividend increase once a year as a reward for sticking with the plan.

This again, requires that we think of our portfolio as a small side business. When we put in a little extra cash each month, we get more dividends. We're not earning more on the same money, but we're growing our side business and getting a bigger paycheck. So it's a raise.

You can chart your increasing income instead of your volatile account balance. Watching your paycheck increase with each investment reinforces the behavior we want to encourage. How many raises can you expect each year? $1 + 4 + 12 \rightarrow 17$ raises a year—and that's *per company* you invest in. And, if you have a retirement account or are not doing any optional cash purchases, that's still five raises a year just for "hanging out." That's 17 opportunities to celebrate for each company you own. Instead of the dread that arrives with each statement, now each statement arrives with a raise. Crazy simple, but trust me, really effective.

An opportunity to celebrate is also an opportunity to talk with your spouse or family about your wealth-building progress. As I mentioned in the book's Preface, of the most common sources of marriage tension is money. While celebrating may not relieve the tension entirely, it at least provides an opportunity to balance it with some happiness. It provides a positive way to connect over money, rather than the unpleasant experience many have.

It gets better.

If you're up for tracking a few transactions in a spreadsheet, we can forecast your raise and use that forecast to enjoy the anticipation of success.

I experienced this phenomenon with my toddler. If we wake up one morning and go to the zoo, he'll enjoy it. If instead I tell him for a week that we're planning a trip to the zoo, by the time zoo-day arrives he's up early, dressed, and excited to get out the door.

Anticipation is a great tool to eke out extra enjoyment. Research even shows that the largest boost of happiness when taking a vacation is from the planning process.

And, it gets even better.

Your raise is going to be between 7-15%. A year.

Are you getting a 10% raise at your job? Even a 7% raise? Yeah, me neither. But my elephant is—and yours will too. I hope your ego can handle that.

### 3. Beat inflation
Another important aspect of your raise is beating inflation.

Keeping cash around for an emergency is important. However, as an investment strategy, it's a losing proposition.

We all have used a phrase similar: "remember when I was a kid and it only cost ¢50 a gallon for gas?". If you kept a dollar in your pocket from when you were a kid and pulled up today to fill your car with gas, you wouldn't get very far.

That's how inflation works—prices increase over time. The government has a target for healthy inflation. It's greater than zero. Which means cash becomes devalued over the natural course of time.

Your investment strategy must grow your capital faster than inflation in order to make forward progress towards improving your financial situation. The Elephant's Paycheck helps you get ahead because that 7-15% raise will beat inflation handily. And, unlike your "real" job, your elephant won't hit a career plateau and stop getting raises. Your elephant won't get laid off.

Later on, you're going to do an exercise where you look at some companies and find out how much they've raised dividends, on average, over the past five years. Even if you stopped reinvesting dividends (because you wanted to spend them) and didn't do optional cash purchases, you'd still get the annual raises uncovered by your research. The reinvested dividends and optional cash purchases accelerate your raises, but aren't the only component of them. You will learn when you do your research that even those one-time-per-year dividend raises will beat inflation.

With this plan, you're getting wealthier faster than things are getting more expensive. The importance of beating inflation can't be understated.

### 4. Reduce risk

We've been taught when it comes to investing that if the rewards sound too good to be true, we should not trust them. At best, we've learned that with better returns come bigger risk.

Both these truisms are, in fact, true. However, neither one accounts for real-world human nature.

There's a great comparison to stock market prices. Why do some companies announce great results, only to have their stock price fall—while others earn much less but get rewarded with a stock price jump?

You might hear an answer along the lines of "expectations". You can look at past performance and value the past "scientifically" because, well, it's already happened. So facts can be used to value the company. But, projecting the future is a bit more uncertain.

Analysts have expectations. They hold companies to different standards. It's a human game. And that's why it's hard to understand. It's not based on *facts*; it's based on experience and gut and creating a model is that can be used to forecast a company's value.

And it seems to make no sense at all. Because it's human.

I propose that we can make the same claim about Dividend Aristocrats and risk. While mathematically, past dividend increase behavior doesn't change the risk profile, it *absolutely* tells us about the company's intent—about their discipline, their priorities, and their process. A company doesn't increase dividends for 25 years or more *accidentally*.

Even the CEO's ego comes into play. I mentioned this before, but it's worth repeating—would *you* want to be the person who broke the 25 year, or 50 year, or more streak for dividend increases? I certainly wouldn't.

This indicates that there's a purpose and a set of processes and priorities to support that purpose. This is something we, as investors, can bank on.

### 5. Track your success

Considering dividend raises and the perspective of the Elephant's Paycheck instead of the size of the elephant, we created four custom metrics as part of the blueprint:

1. The Elephant's Paycheck

2. The elephant's projected raise

3. Actual cost (considering your portfolio as a side business, not a set of investment transactions)

4. Actual return (considering the effect of time and compounding on your actual cost; again, from the perspective of running a side business not managing an investment portfolio)

We'll get into these metrics, at least the ones we've not yet talked about, at the end of this part. These metrics are important, as they provide a unique perspective on the progress you're making. They help inform your decision-making process around everything from what investments to make (before you make them) to what news to pay attention to and what to ignore (after you do).

You won't see these on your brokerage statement, so we'll help you keep track of them if you'd like. You can choose to monitor these metrics with each transaction—each dividend raise, dividend reinvestment, and optional cash purchase—or at any point in time to understand how far you've come.

Tracking and reflecting on your progress is empowering. It helps you keep perspective on how far you've come and reminds you as to why you're making the effort in the first place. It reinforces your habits, provides an opportunity to celebrate your success, and helps build even more mastery to increase your satisfaction.

In short—tracking your progress helps to keep you motivated.

## 6. Stay motivated

Just like the companies we own have processes and priorities around increasing the dividend, we also have our own processes and priorities to help us stay focused on what matters. That focus keeps us motivated because we have made a clear decision on what matters to us, and just as importantly—what doesn't.

An investing plan that doesn't help you stay motivated is missing a crucial element required for long-term success. The best plan isn't going to do very much for investors that opt-out for lack of interest.

It's difficult not to look at your portfolio value as a measure of success. As discussed earlier, we replace that metric with the Elephant's Paycheck as a way to give us something more interesting to measure—something designed to keep us motivated.

And it sure is motivating to watch your paycheck grow.

I created a sample portfolio when I started writing this book, one that mirrors the portfolio I setup for my wife. The resulting Elephant's Paycheck is up just under 50% in the three years and three months since starting that portfolio. Simply sticking with the plan (that doesn't include optional cash purchases, only annual dividend raises and quarterly dividend reinvestments), we conservatively project a raise over 11% for the next year.

Sticking with the plan brings to bear one of the most powerful tools at our disposal: time.

### 7. Focus on time, not timing

In any situation, always look for your natural advantage. Sun Tzu probably said something like that about warfare—and it's true for investing as well.

The natural advantage for the individual investor is time. The process through which we leverage time is compounding.

As time goes by, each dividend we've earned in the past and reinvested is also earning its own dividend. That's the meaning of compounding.

Compounding adds up faster than most people assume. It's why the sample portfolio results we saw a few paragraphs ago, the roughly 50% raise, might seem shocking. This is truly the manifestation of your money earning money. Compounding is a very powerful tool when combined with our perspective on the Elephant's Paycheck.

A great thing about compounding is that it works the same *regardless of how much you have invested*—because it's based on percentages, not absolute values. The growth percentage you'll achieve by investing $1,000 is exactly the same as the growth percentage you'll achieve by investing a million dollars.

Of course, it requires some amount of patience to see the results—and that's where people lose interest. However, once the value of compounding sinks in, you'll really start to get excited by your Elephant's Paycheck raises. Especially when you realize you don't need to "stay on top the market" and worry about how every bit of news affects your results.

Realizing this, you reduce your investing anxiety, and the satisfaction that comes with deliberate progress can take over.

Have you ever run a race, or started a hard project like a home remodel, only to hit that point where you think—"what have I gotten myself into?!". But you persist, and you come out the other side of that doubt with great satisfaction. Even before you're finished the race or the project, you get a burst of confidence once you recognize that what you need to do is not beyond your capability. Setbacks slide off your shoulders. You know you are on the right track.

The equivalent of that moment for the Elephant's Paycheck is when you realize the raises are going to keep coming, and that compounding is your friend. It's a moment you should celebrate. You'll deserve it.

## 8. Avoid information overload

When you have a clear plan, understanding as well what to do as what not to do, you can be deliberate in how you consume information.

The price of oil? Don't care.

Unemployment? Don't care.

Interest rates? Don't care.

Watching financial news can make you crazy with fear, uncertainty, and doubt (FUD). FUD leads to bad decision-making, or worse—giving up on your commitment to create a safe financial future.

Just stick to the plan. Put your elephant to work, reinvest his earnings, and let his paycheck compound. Pay attention to your investments. Get to know your companies in an intimate way, one that comes with time and thought.

Let's say you've graduated from college and managed to save your first thousand dollars. That money represents your whole life savings—and it's all that's left from the hard work of getting your degree and the labor you've traded for your paycheck.

**... yet your balance is lower than when you started at the end of some months, even though you added money that month. How rewarding does that feel?**

Why would you invest your life's savings that in a company whose CEO you couldn't even name, or one whose products you couldn't tell a friend about—products that don't even excite or interest you?

Think about it this way: chances are you've done an online search of some of the people you've dated. But have you googled the CEO of the company's you've invested in? *Why not?*

Take care, and pay attention to what matters. The Elephant's Paycheck gives you a framework for understanding what matters and what to ignore. Over time, this leads to a deeper understanding of your companies, how they're doing, and what matters to their continued success.

In part four, I'll share a list of things to do to keep tabs on in your companies so that you can make better decisions without getting sucked into the vortex of FUD that financial news tends to create.

Of course, even some non-financial news will be relevant to your investment strategy.

### 9. Align to your social values

A while back, it came out that the CEO of a popular internet company was an elephant-killing hunter.

*How does this make you feel?*

A top food company regularly tortures chicks.

*Offended? Why would you invest in the company?*

Think fracking is bad for the environment? What about "too big to fail banks"?

*Are these the kind of activities you want your company participating in?*

When you invest in the company, you're an owner. It's your company.

Do these activities—hunting, animal testing, fracking, big-banks—represent your values? Maybe they do—but if they don't, *why would you invest in them?*

More and more, customers are choosing companies that take a stand in support of their core values. Investors should too—for the same reasons. It's not because your small investment choices will change the world. It's because together we can make a difference. If we all just operated in alignment to our values all the time—as consumers, as investors, and as employees—we'd really start to affect positive change in the world.

When you invest in mutual funds, you don't get to pick the companies in the fund. *So how can you be sure that you're investing in alignment with your values when you invest blindly in funds?* You can't.

There are funds that focus on socially responsible companies, but those funds typically have higher costs because they're actively managed. They also aren't index funds.

Much of the value of mutual funds to modest long-term investors is keeping costs down and matching the performance of an index. But when you lose both those value points, mutual funds seem a lot less compelling.

*Why not choose a plan like the Elephant's Paycheck Blueprint where you can invest wisely—and in alignment with your personal values?*

## 10. Be empowered

Your life. Your money. Your choices.

You're in control, and it feels good.

You're establishing mastery, you have a plan, and you're tracking your progress.

Empowerment gives you confidence and keeps you motivated. It helps you build wealth and achieve financial safety. It's a crucial human element of an investing blueprint.

THE ELEPHANT IN THE ROOM HAS A PAYCHECK

## METRICS AND PERSPECTIVE

The Elephant's Paycheck Blueprint is a long-term investing plan. Along with the why's and the how's, we've created some metrics to track your progress that also keep you encouraged and enjoying the process. Crucial to understanding why these metrics accurately reflect your progress, but aren't on your brokerage statement, is the perspective we take and the resulting underlying assumptions our perspective rests upon.

- That you're starting a small business, not managing a portfolio

- That your brokerage statement is driven by IRS compliance/reporting

- That your statement is not designed emotionally, just factually in the context of taxes and transaction reporting

Think about the story you'd tell if your elephant were starting a business in your garage and he was a sole proprietor. In this context, let's consider the four metrics we want to track.

### 1. The Elephant's Paycheck, not his size

We've discussed the birth of the metaphor and the meaning of the paycheck; however, it's also worth understanding some of the backstory.

*Why don't brokerages think this way? Why does the size of the elephant usually have such a hold on the way we perceive building wealth?*

Partly, it's because this is a natural way to think about money and our progress saving it—and another reason is because it's necessary for reporting the right information to the IRS (both individually and as an institution that has to comply with the laws of the land).

Natural or not, it plays to the way money works. After all, we have to pay taxes, so we have to know how much the portfolio grew. And so a whole set of assumptions and stories arise from the decision to pay attention to portfolio value.

The limits of focusing on the elephant's size are especially obvious when it comes to retirement planning. Instead of tracking the portfolio's income with an eye towards matching income to spending in retirement, people still use their balance as the indicator of progress.

Have a look at your most recent statement. The one thing you're sure to see right on the front page is current balance and change from last month (as if a one-month change was indicative of anything relevant to your long-term plan). Monitoring online isn't much better. My bank shows me my balance, how much it's changed today, and my one-year rate of return (how much my balance has changed in the last year) right on the top of every page.

Even though my investment strategy is based on dividend income, the only place I can see my expected dividend income is buried nine pages deep on my monthly statement. It's not available at all online. The funny thing is that the brokerage asked me what I care about when I opened my account. Even though I told them that I care about income, they still primarily judge my success based on my balance and balance-related metrics (and not my income and income-related metrics). What your brokerage shows will vary from mine, but probably reflects similar priorities of your financial institution—that portfolio balance is what matters most.

As a result, when it comes to retirement planning, people tend to follow a rule of thumb about how much you can withdraw from your retirement account each year. It amazes me though, since so many assumptions need to be made that the "calculations" seem worthless to me—or at least, highly prone to error.

Let's think about some of the assumptions. You might often hear that you can safely withdraw 3% (or 4%, or 5%) of your retirement savings each year and not run out of money. This calculation is based on how long you expect to live, your expected lifestyle, your expected medical bills, what inflation will be for the next 20 or 30 years, and so on. As we know, predicting the future is quite hard—and trying to determine how things will pan out in the years to come can add a lot of worry. What if you ~~guessed~~ predicted wrong? The Elephant's Paycheck Blueprint makes the worrying unnecessary because it helps you focus on your income just like you do when you're not retired.

Back to the metaphor—account balance is like the size of the elephant. If things get bad and you need to eat the elephant, it's good to have a big one. More importantly though, for retirement planning or improving your quality of life, is how much that elephant can earn (before you need to resort to cooking him).

We look at the income the elephant generates separately from how big he is and how much he is growing. It's not a complete picture, because the elephant will likely get bigger over time. The elephant's growth is just gravy.

Focusing on the paycheck prevents you from having to worry if you have enough money to do something. You can treat investing just like working (without the actual work part). You see what your income is and can determine a standard of living based on your priorities.

As a side note, dividend income is taxed at a lower rate than normal paycheck income. As a result, it's worth more than regular income because you give less away to the government.

Your Elephant's Paycheck is a more natural measure of your wealth because it's easily translated into your standard of living. It's simpler to plan around the paycheck than it is to plan around the size of the elephant.

### 2. The Elephant's raises, both past and projected

The metaphor works really well as a way to understand all aspects of the blueprint. If the elephant is working, he's going to want a raise. As outlined earlier, the raises are valuable. They're consistent, they're frequent—and they're pretty significant.

The Elephant's Paycheck blueprint tracks two raises.

The simple one is the raise we've already received. Quite easy to track, it's simply the difference in the paycheck size over a period of time. If you commit to tracking things monthly, you can visualize each step along the way. Or, simply track your starting point and add up all your dividend amounts at any point in time to see how much it's grown.

In part two chapter four, Reinvesting Dividends, we had an example that tracked a fictional stock share purchase for a year. In that example, we achieved an 8.3% raise after one year.

To summarize the same example, we started with a $1,000 investment in a company with a 3% dividend yield. Meaning, this investment paid $30 in dividends a year. To simplify the example, we assumed that the stock price didn't change all year. We reinvested the 3% dividend quarterly. At the end of the year the reinvestments resulted in a total investment value of $1,031.36.

We then assumed a reasonable 5% dividend increase, making the total yield 3.15% (3.15% is a 5% increase on 3%) resulting in a total dividend of $32.49 (3.15% x $1.031.36).

Said in plain English, at the start of the year we were earning $30/year in dividends. At the end, we were earning $32.49. A $2.49 increase on $30 reflects an 8.3% raise.

That's the first raise tracked, the accomplishment over the past. As each year goes on, you will track the total raise you've received over time.

There's also the possibility to "easily" forecast your projected raise for the upcoming year. It requires tracking each reinvestment and the last annual raise for each company you own in a spreadsheet. While it's not something we'll cover in this book, you can see it, along with past raise tracking, online in the sample portfolio (at http://ElephantsPaycheck.com/sample-portfolio). From that same location, you can also download templates to use for your own portfolio.

### 3. Actual cost, not cost basis

Here's where the perspective of owning a small business really kicks in and adds value.

Pretend you've taken some money and started a small business on the side. Imagine the story you'd tell after you achieved the brilliant success that I'm sure you'd earn. It might go something like this:

"I was so convinced to do this, that I took my last $1,000 and invested it in materials to launch the product. I ate nothing but cans of soup for months until we actually made money, but even then I put most of what we were earning back in the business so we could get more customers and grown even faster."

You would *not* say:

"I was so convinced to do this that I took my last $1,000 and invested it in materials to launch the product. The first year we earned only $2,000, and the second just $5,000—which in both years we reinvested in the business to grow while we lived off my wife's paycheck. So I guess you could say we started the business with $8,000."

However, the latter scenario is exactly how people think about their portfolios. It's because the IRS is transactional, and your brokerage has to comply with IRS regulations on reporting stock transactions.

Each dividend reinvestment is actually considered two transactions—a dividend distribution and a stock purchase. Each of those transactions is related to the tax you'll owe from investing activities. But they don't reflect your *actual progress* towards building wealth.

If you take the perspective of a small business owner and think about the money you started with, all the reinvestments simply look like business growth—not cost accrual.

Let me give you an example.

Let's say you invest $1,000 in a company that pays a 3% dividend that you reinvest. For simplicity, let's ignore the potential of company stock price appreciation and assume the dividend is paid annually so that we don't have to calculate the effect of compounding for this example. At the end of the first year, you would have received and reinvested $30 in dividends. Your total investment in the company would be valued at $1,030.

The IRS would say that you haven't grown because the IRS looks at the reinvestment as a new investment. You invested $1,030 and are worth $1,030. In IRS terms, your cost basis is $1,030 comprised of the initial $1,000 investment and the additional $30 in dividends that you invested. From a "how much tax do I owe" perspective, this is rational logic.

But from a wealth-building perspective—maybe not so much. You started with $1,000. You now have $1,030. You're ahead by 3% from where you started without any additional out-of-pocket capital (cost) invested into your "business".

Actual cost is different from your cost basis in that we only count the amount you take out of your pocket and put into "the business" (for example, through optional cash purchases). We can use it as a measure of progress and success, though of course you still need to track your cost basis and pay your taxes if you're not working with a retirement account.

### 4. Actual yield, not dividend yield

Dividend yield, if you recall, is the dividend payment over the price of the stock. The dividend yield reflects the current stock price.

It's useful to consider dividend yield when evaluating a company for purchase or sale of stock. It's less useful as a measure of the value of an existing investment in a company.

The existing investment used a certain amount of capital (your Actual Cost). That capital is now returning your dividend. The Actual Yield you're receiving is the dividend as a percentage of your Actual Cost, not the current stock price. At least from the perspective of building a business.

Continuing the previous example: the $1,020 investment you have in the company pays a dividend of $20.40, assuming it hasn't been increased like it would be for a Dividend Aristocrat.

The dividend yield remains 2% (by definition—we haven't changed the stock price or the dividend payout). The math is $20.40/$1,020 = 2\%$.

However, the Actual Yield on your initial investment to get your business up and started is $20.40/$1,000 = 2.04\%$.

This perspective provides yet another reason for the value of sticking with your plan over a longer period of time. The Actual Yield will increase over time, reflecting the reinvestments and dividend increases that work for you but don't add to your Actual Cost. Actual Yield is often called 'yield on cost' by the establishment but it's not used very prominently.

I like this metric because it places a value on the length of time you've been sticking to your plan. As investors, we know using time works to our advantage, but it's all lip-service unless we're actually measuring the impact it has on our results.

### 5. Using this example to look at the paycheck and the raise

It's worth looking at how this example plays out for the paycheck and the raise.

After the first year, your income would have risen to $20.40 (a 2% increase)—that is, at least in this simple example. It would have risen a little bit more in your real-world portfolio due to compounding and the annual dividend increase you can expect from Dividend Aristocrats.

If your Dividend Aristocrats increase their dividend by 5% (you'll do research in part four to see what the real-world ranges are), then you'd have over a 7% increase: 2% from reinvesting, a fraction of a percent from compounding, and 5% from the annual increase.

### 6. Absolute values versus percentages

Let's talk about one final perspective shift you need to make, that of absolute values versus percentage values.

In our example, you received slightly more than a 7% raise over the year. Sounds great, right?

Except that 7% of the original $20 paycheck is just $1.40.

You got a $1.40 raise—which doesn't sound as great as 7%.

This is another reason it's hard to stay motivated. Creating the blueprint and making the sacrifices to invest $1,000 all take energy—energy that in the end returned only $1.40. Not even enough for a cup of coffee.

It can be depressing to think in absolute dollar amounts, and so you must shift to also considering percentages in order to stay on track.

The reality is that we have what we have to invest. If we had more, the absolute amounts would certainly change—but *the percentages would be exactly the same.* Because of compounding and the value we put on time (rather than timing), these percentages really work to our favor to maximize our wealth building efforts.

## JUST DO IT

I always thought the big difference between telling a good story and writing a helpful book is the ability to give people the confidence to get started.

You will feel different after you make your first investment if you've never invested before. If you have, some of part four will be familiar and maybe even unnecessary.

Part of gaining confidence and developing mastery is a clear plan for getting started and keeping going.

That's what you'll find in part four. I make the assumption that you've never invested before so that anyone can get started. Then, with step-by-step instructions, you'll learn to evaluate and buy the companies you want to own. Just like when I wrote in the beginning of the book that I'd use absolute language at times when in the real world it's really not so absolute, I do the same here.

There are many ways to actually make your investments— especially today, where you can download mobile apps that allow you to buy stocks easily (though perhaps not cheaply).

The benefits of the approach I describe in the next section are that it's really easy to do and I know will work the same way for a long time to come. It will also minimize your fees and support building a healthy investing habit.

The approach below accomplishes everything I hope for you, and that's really what matters—that you get started and build mastery.

Odds are that by this point, you're wondering:

*How do I actually buy stock?*

*What can I do to learn more once I've made my first investment?*

*How do I track my progress?*

Let's jump into part four's step-by-step instructions that answer all these questions and more.

PART

4

# Putting Your Plan Into Action

I've shared the backstory, the metaphor, and a way to shift perspective and achieve a deeper understanding of managing a portfolio for building wealth. So far, this book has focused on the theory. Now it's time to start taking some action.

This is where I feel many books fail, because they're not prescriptive enough.

Even if you've never invested before, I hope that you can follow this part and have your elephant earning some dough by the time you finish.

One caveat, however: I'm going to recommend direct stock purchase plans instead of a brokerage account or a mobile app. While using a brokerage may present some advantages, it's not the cheapest solution. It's also not easy for people with modest amounts to invest to get started or set aside small amounts monthly. Mobile apps come and go. There's nothing relevant to the Elephant's Paycheck that you can do on an app that you can't easily do with direct stock purchase plans.

Direct purchase plans have a minimum investment amount. It's commonly $250, though you might find some plans with $100 or $500 minimums. When you invest using direct purchase plans, you invest with "dollar amounts" not "share amounts". Instead of having to purchase some number of shares, you can simply purchase $250 worth of company stock. Direct purchase plans manage the fractional shares for you. This value cannot be overstated for modest investors. It really lowers the cost barrier to entry for young investors.

However, all of the information in this part is easily portable to an online brokerage account or an app should you prefer, or if you're rolling over a 401(k) to an IRA.

Let's get into it. There are four simple steps:

1. Pick a company
2. Make your first investment
3. Create reinforcing habits
4. Do it again

You'll need the Investment Selection Worksheet. You might also find the tracking template spreadsheet valuable. Both documents are available at http://ElephantsPaycheck.com/book-notes. Each contains its own instructions. If you can't get online right now, the next section has a sample of a completed worksheet that you can use to follow along.

## 1. PICK A COMPANY

It's a great idea to spend some time thinking about the companies you do business with. Most won't be public companies, or have dividends.

In the course I created for job switchers—people who need help rolling over their 401(k) into an IRA and creating an Elephant's Paycheck Blueprint—many really enjoyed the exercise of tracking companies with whom they did business. It's a mindful approach to selecting companies in which to invest, because the process kicks off a very personal way of thinking about companies. The personalization of the company that you're researching transfers over even when you're researching companies with which you don't share that same familiarity.

So take a personal view of the company you're researching. Ask yourself how it would feel as you imagine doing business with them. Look at news that's less about random financial statistics (like how the price of oil impacts travel companies—which would already be priced into stock prices by the professionals) and more about what people are saying about the companies.

There are so many connections we can make to these companies. Maybe you like (or dislike) their products? Or you like (or dislike)

> ## Instead of having to purchase some number of shares, you can simply purchase $250 worth of company stock.

what they stand for? That's one of the great things about the free market: you can speak with your actions and choose to invest in successful companies that you also admire. When you have a personal connection to the company, the products, or the mission, you'll stay better informed and more engaged with your investments.

It's especially fun for kids to own a company whose products they use. Try taking your child to the supermarket to see their P&G or 3M product, or to visit "their" AT&T, Target, or Walmart store. (Yes, each of those companies is a Dividend Aristocrat.)

One family who started an Elephant's Paycheck Blueprint with their kids shared their experience with me. After buying Exxon stock, their kids insisted at filling up at "their gas station" instead of the discount alternatives. Every lesson has a price, even sometimes for the parents.

Our purpose here is to narrow down our choices to a single company. You can pick more than one, and in fact, probably should. (But we'll talk more about that in step four.)

I've created a worksheet to help you track the details about the companies you consider. It will also help you get familiar with important elements of stock market investing. There certainly are more aspects of companies to evaluate. When you are getting started it's important to avoid too much complexity so that we keep the barrier to getting started low. It's a balance, and the worksheet represents the balance I've chosen for the Elephant's Paycheck Blueprint.

Make some notes on this worksheet as you take the steps below. Use it to help you compare companies to each other and decide which make better investments for you and your family.

Here is a sample of a completed worksheet:

---

## INVESTMENT SELECTION WORKSHEET

---

### Section 1: Basic Company Information

Company Name:__P&G__(Proctor & Gamble)__
Ticker Symbol:__PG__
Sector: consumer staples

### Section 2: Company Dividend Profile

Current stock price:__76.81__
Current dividend amount:__$2.64__
Current dividend yield:__3.44%__
Dividend payout as % of earnings:__87.22%__
5-year Dividend growth rate:__6.59%__

What months/dates are the dividend paid?__Feb/May/Aug/Nov__
When do the dividend increases occur (which month?)__April__

Look at the list of Dividend Aristocrats (http://ElephantsPaycheck. com/dividend-aristocrats) and see if any catch your eye. There are likely some companies that you'll recognize, so start with those.

The first thing to do is to check out their websites to see if they have a direct purchase plan. Usually, you'll find it under the investors section of the website. For example, have a look at http:// pg.com/. Right at the top left, you'll see a link for "Investor/shareholder relations". Selecting that link will take you to a page that lists "Individual Investor Information" which gives you all the information you'll need to get started if you choose to invest in P&G. If you can't find it, try the FAQ (frequently asked questions) section. Even if you're cheating and not picking a Dividend Aristocrat for your investment, I've seen companies answer the "can I purchase stock directly from the company" question in the FAQ.

Next, check out the news section of the shareholder website. There's no need for interpretation of what's said, because companies write their own press releases and tell you what they're doing in plain English. Do you agree with their justifications and with their direction?

If there's a shareholder email newsletter, subscribe. GE has started accepting and answering individual investor questions in the newsletter following earnings, and I wouldn't be surprised if more companies begin the same practice.

Download and read the company's most recent annual report, particularly the letter to shareholders. You'll find this at the beginning of every annual report, and it's written in plain English. For example, you can find P&G's Annual Report on the financial reporting page of the investor website. It's even helpful to read the letters from a few years back, as it will give you a sense of the company's strategic trajectory.

To get some understanding of the financials, look for the quarterly earnings announcements. You can find these in the press release section of the investor site. These releases are becoming clearer and easier to understand, and provide a good list of material events relative to the business.

I suggest listening to the quarterly earnings conference call recordings. These calls are usually structured with an executive giving a business update, followed by financials. The call is then opened up to questions from professional analysts. It's a great way to get insight into the company. You'd likely find these recordings on an events page on the investor site.

As you can see, it's a good idea to become familiar with your company's investor sites and the tools available for you to keep on top of your company.

You can complete the worksheet for as many companies as you'd like; it's good exercise. But we're only looking for one investment at this step.

Pick your top investment choice and let's go on to the next step—where you'll actually make the investment.

## 2. MAKE YOUR FIRST INVESTMENT

Now that you've selected your company, head to its investor website.

The company will either have a packet of information available for download or will have a link to the site that does. You can sign up online for some plans; for others, you need to print out and send in paperwork (and a check).

Follow the instructions, which tend to be pretty easy. You will need a social security number for the person who will own the shares. If you're setting this up as a gift, you will need the recipient's social security number (not yours). If the recipient is a minor, you'll need to setup an adult custodian whose social security number you will need as well.

In addition to the social security number, all you'll need to get started are address, phone number, and email address. If you sign up online, you'll need your checking account information so that you can make a digital money transfer. The information you need (bank routing number and checking account number) are always found on the bottom your bank checks (in the United States).

Once you've submitted the paperwork (either online or via postal mail), you'll get confirmation through postal mail. At that time, you'll also receive information on how to access your online account where you can view transactions and statements, and setup optional cash purchases.

Three minor technical aspects of investing online:

1. If you sign up online, before you enter any personal information, make sure that you type the URL using https:// rather than http:// and that you see a small padlock icon in the address bar. This ensures that your personal information is secure and encrypted.

**Many really enjoyed the exercise of tracking companies with whom they did business.**

2. Make sure to bookmark the site you sign up with, and keep track of your username and password.

3. Use an email address that you will always be able to access. For example, don't use your work address. If you switch jobs, you may lose track of important notifications and may not be able to reset your password if you lose it.

You've taken your first step to wealth, and the exciting world of stock market investing. And you're doing it on your terms with a plan to succeed. It doesn't get any better.

## 3. REINFORCE GOOD HABITS

We can't stop with the initial investment, though. If you invest and forget, doubt will eat away at you in the background. You'll always wonder if you're on track, doing the right thing. You'll have a bias towards action, simply for the sake of action rather than in alignment to a plan.

So, we'll create three habits to help us keep focused on our plan and grow your mastery.

1. Create a calendar of important dates.

2. Follow news that matters (and ignore the rest).

3. Track your progress.

### 1. Create a calendar

Set up a new calendar on your computer with entries only related to your Elephant's Paycheck. In all calendar programs, you will see an option to create a new calendar, not just a new event. Select the option to create a new calendar. (When prompted for a calendar name, why not call it 'Elephant's Paycheck'?)

Creating a new calendar has some advantages over adding your Elephant's Paycheck events to your normal calendar. You can show or hide all the events in the calendar to manage calendar clutter. You can also share it with your family or investing club to better communicate your investing blueprint and activities towards mastery.

Add the following dates into this calendar:

1. Create a recurring quarterly event for **dividend payments**.

2. Create a recurring annual event for the **dividend raise**.

3. Create a recurring quarterly event for earnings reports.

It's often not possible to put the exact date in the calendar, because the dates will vary based on how the calendar falls out in each year. For dividend payments, you might put the alert at the end of the payment month. This way, the alert will also serve as a reminder to check your account statement and update your tracker (we'll get to that in a little bit).

Do that same for dividend raises: schedule the notifications at the end of the month you expect the raise. When you're reminded about the raise, you'd go to the investor website news section to see the press release that mentions the raise.

Put the quarterly earnings events at the beginning of the month, so that you can make sure to update your calendar with the earnings call information and listen to the call in real time if you choose.

Make sure that each of these calendar events is setup to notify you appropriately.

## 2. Follow news that matters

It is important to stay in touch with your company. However, traditional financial news has become quite fear-driven, and usually doesn't provide much value for the individual investor who's thinking long-term. It's a good idea to stay away from that financial news on TV.

PUTTING YOUR PLAN INTO ACTION

However, most of the companies themselves put out great information. Definitely head over to the investor site and sign up for the shareholder email newsletter. The newsletter will also notify you of earnings events and dividend information, which is helpful to make sure you didn't enter it into your calendar incorrectly or overlook the calendar notifications.

Keep an eye on the investor site's new section too. While it may not be your only source of information about the company, it's a good starting point to learn about key activities and market happenings. If it's offered, set up company news alerts on the investor site.

As discussed elsewhere, listen to the earnings calls and read the letter to shareholders in the annual earnings report.

### 3. Track your progress
A few key elements to tracking your progress:

1. Note your starting point. Specifically, track the number of shares you purchased, your purchase price, and the dividend on the date of purchase.

2. Make sure to download your statements quarterly and keep your own copy. Most companies will keep these statements available, but it's always best to have your own copy. At the end of the year, you can keep just the annual summary. When you first get started, make sure that dividends are being reinvested properly. Should you move your home, make sure to update the account address.

3. You can download templates created for the Elephant's Paycheck blueprint at http://ElephantsPaycheck.com/sample-portfolio.

## 4. REPEAT
There are many reasons to build an Elephant's Paycheck Blueprint. Maybe you've switched jobs and want to know what to do with your 401(k) rollover. Or you've just entered the workforce and

want to learn how to invest. Perhaps you're a parent who wants a program to teach your kids about investing and financial responsibility, or grandparents who'd like to bond with your grandchildren and pass along some of your experience.

Grandparents and parents working with their children should stick with one company. It keeps focus on the ownership of the company, what you can learn about how the public markets work, and what it means to invest and save for the future. You accomplish your objectives with a single company.

Job switchers are going to be using a brokerage and probably will have a relatively large sum of money to invest. You definitely want between three and five, or more companies to make sure that you have some diversity.

If you're just starting to learn about investing, you should also consider more than one company. My recommendation is three. And, all other things considered, pick the three companies such that each is on a different dividend payment schedule. This way, you'll get a dividend payment (and reinvestment raise!) each month. This might seem like a strange way to pick a stock, but the benefit to doing so is building the habit. A reinvestment and raise each month trains our brains into a consistent habit of caring about the Elephant's Paycheck, not his size.

You shouldn't underestimate the fun of getting a raise every single month. Even though the raises will be small when you start out, reinforcing healthy investing habits will help keep you on the right path.

What's seemingly similarly strange but similarly valuable is (all other things considered) to pick companies with dividend raises in *different months*. I don't believe it's possible to get dividend raises every month; there are a couple of months that simply don't have a Dividend Aristocrat that offers a dividend increase. However, you should be able to get dividend raises nine or ten months of the year. These raises will be larger than your reinvestment raises, and you'll get them even when you stop reinvesting dividends.

> **It's especially fun for kids to own a company whose products they use. Try taking your child to the supermarket to see their P&G or 3M product, or to visit "their" AT&T, Target, or Walmart store.**

The only practical thing to consider other than dividend timing when you're evaluating multiple companies is the company's sector and industry. Keep your investments in different sectors, for example one company in consumer staples (Procter & Gamble), one in industrials (Dover Corp), and one in financials (Cincinnati Financial).

By spreading your investments across multiple sectors, you try to ensure that they're not all subject to the same economic factors, like weather or unemployment levels. You can imagine that energy companies don't make as much money when people don't heat or cool their house. A cool summer or warm winter affects the whole industry. Similarly, when unemployment is high, people stay away from premium products (like those from P&G) and stick with generic or bulk brands (like Walmart). Said differently, market sectors move in cycles. If you diversify, you work to avoid multiple investments having down parts of the cycle at the same time. This is an over-simplistic way of thinking about diversification. However, considering that you're just getting started, I feel it's a point of view that's both approachable and actionable.

To pick multiple companies, you'd just repeat the process above until you've picked all the companies you need (and as explained in the worksheet). Repeat steps two and three until you have each of your company's setup.

The investment selection worksheet walks you through these steps and has a page to summarize your findings and compare the different companies. Here's an example of one filled out:

## Dividend Plan Comparison Summary Worksheet

| | Procter & Gamble | Dover Corp | Cincinnati Financial |
|---|---|---|---|
| NAME | Procter & Gamble | Dover Corp | Cincinnati Financial |
| TICKER | PG | DOV | CINF |
| SECTOR | consumer staples | industrials | financials |
| MIN STARTING INVESTMENT | $250 | $500 or $50 automatic | $25 |
| INITIAL PURCHASE FEE | $0 | $10 | $0 |
| REINVESTMENT FEE | paid by company | 5% up tp $3 + $0.12 per share purchased | $0 |
| OPTIONAL PURCHASE FEE | $0 if automatic, or $2.50 if not | $0.12 per share purchased | $0 |
| OPTIONAL PURCHASE MIN | $50 | $50 | $25 |
| CURRENT PRICE | $76.81 | $52.60 | $54.42 |
| CURRENT DIVIDEND | $2.64 | $1.68 | $1.84 |
| CURRENT YIELD | 3.44% | 3.19% | 3.38% |
| PAYOUT RATIO | 87.22% | 43.08% | 47.06% |
| 5 YEAR DIVIDEND GROWTH | 6.59% | 8.84% | 2.83% |
| DIVIDEND MONTHS | Feb/May/Aug/Nov | Mar/Jun/Sep/Dec | Jan/Apr/Jul/Oct |
| DIVIDEND RAISE MONTH | April | August | January |

There are a few things to notice on this completed sheet:

1. The fees for each program vary, as do the minimum required to get started.

2. Dover has high fees, but has a great history of dividend raises with 8.84% five-year dividend growth. Do you think they'll continue? Check out their low payout ratio, it indicates that they can continue with their raises. If you think they can keep up the raises, maybe the fees are worth paying?

3. Cincinnati Financial has a very low entry point with just $25 required to get started. They clearly value this program and are making it accessible. Even though they have a low dividend growth recently, the low fees and low dollar amount required to get started make it a great plan for kids.

4. Each of these companies is on a different dividend payment schedule, so with these three companies you'd get a dividend every month of the year.

# Conclusion

I hope you took your time with this part and are now the proud owner of your first company (or more). I'm excited for you. This is a first step, a small step—but it marks the beginning of a great adventure.

It can be tedious to keep up with all the activity, but it is worth it. Why update spreadsheets when you have statements? Well, you don't *have* to. The blueprint will work the same regardless. However, you'll learn more if you take a bit of time each month to make a quick spreadsheet entry for that month's optional cash purchases, dividend reinvestments, and dividend raises.

When people are trying to develop good budgeting and spending habits, there's a practice of using cash. This tends to make you feel more connected to the money you're spending. A $100 purchase doesn't seem like much when you use plastic. It's hard to connect with how much you're actually spending when you swipe a credit card in the same way as you do when counting out the bills.

The Elephant's Paycheck Blueprint works in a similar way. It's easy to just set up the blueprint and put it on autopilot; in fact, that's the whole idea. But to feel your progress more intimately, an entry line or two in a spreadsheet each month can go a long way. When it gets hard to stick to the blueprint, having the connection to the numbers, to your progress, is going to be important. This is when it really makes a difference.

### A personal note

You did it! I'm excited for you; I hope you are too.

You're a stock market investor, and are working your way towards mastery by narrowing your attention in alignment to your objective.

I want you to continue to learn about your companies. Pay attention to the Elephant's Paycheck metrics so that you stay motivated

Make sure to celebrate your progress. Now that you've started, you're going to see progress if you pay attention to the Elephant's Paycheck metrics. Enjoy it. Celebrate it.

Visit http://ElephantsPaycheck.com/book-notes for updates, to download digital versions of the worksheets, and help on your journey towards wealthy living.

Please stay in touch and let me know how it's going, and if I can help. You can reach me anytime at **db@elephantspaycheck.com**. I'll do my best to get back to you personally and in a timely matter.

I'd also love to come speak to your community. If you have enjoyed this book and the way I tell a story, please consider inviting me to speak at your next event.

# About the Author

David Bressler is a tech executive and financial coach. His blueprint for building wealth is used by hundreds of people who have taken his online courses or heard him speak.

Bressler created his first online course after noticing how many smart people know very little about investing. In his courses he helps recent college graduates, freelancers, franchise owners, doctors, lawyers and others turn the stress of managing money into a fun experience with unique metrics designed to motivate healthy investing behavior.

He calls society's failure to address our widespread financial illiteracy the elephant in the room—a problem we know is there but refuse to talk about. A goal of this book is to help people take control of their own financial future by giving the elephant a paycheck—a reference to the dividend payments investors can receive when investing in the stock market.

Bressler earned his MBA from New York University's Stern School of Business. By the time he turned 32 he had earned his financial independence and has since continued to build a successful career helping companies improve their business results with technology. His first love, however, is helping beginning investors fall in love with the idea of money making money, just as he did when he was starting out.

His financial coaching approach is infused by lessons learned after almost 40 years of teaching martial arts and serving as a rescue diver for a decade off the New York and New Jersey coasts. He is detailed without being complicated, knows how to reinforce key points regardless your learning style, and can help you use the power of habit to build lasting change.

Bressler, who still practices martial arts in his rare free time, lives and works in New York City with his wife and two young children. *The Elephant in the Room Has a Paycheck* is his first book.

Made in the USA
Lexington, KY
17 July 2017